No gallbladder diet cookbook

Learn To Eat Right After Gallbladder Removal.

Discover 1000 Days Worth Of Recipes That Will Help You Live A Healthy Life After The Operation I With a 30-Days Meal Plan

Melanie Adams and AMZ Creative Lab

D1319499

Sommario

Introduction

Unlike the heart and the brain, among other organs, the gallbladder is not a mandatory organ that one must have to stay alive and lead a healthy and well-rounded life. However, that doesn't mean that there is absolutely no need to have this organ and that it has zero importance. Elimination of the gallbladder and the possible outcomes of this action will be discussed a little later, but let us first see why the gallbladder is important. This book will discuss everything about the gallbladder diet plus delicious recipes to help you stay healthy and happy. The gallbladder is responsible for pumping bile into the small intestine to aid in digestion. It acts on prompts it receives from the brain and performs its duties, without which digestion is not a very easy process.

This book will teach you everything you need to know about gallstones, how to treat them, how they are diagnosed, and the role your diet plays in preventing and healing gallbladder problems.

Bile, the viscous fluid, comes in a variety of colors. As a result, it is beneficial in fat digestion. Every 24 hours, your liver produces 34 fluid oz of bile.

The liver transports waste from the stomach to the small intestine. Food must be preserved in order to be safe until it is ready to be consumed again. This is where the gallbladder enters the picture.

Bile is stored and concentrated in the gallbladder. It can hold anywhere from 1 to 2.7 fluid oz depending on the type. When you eat fat, your gallbladder empties into your small intestine.

It serves as a storage area for the bile produced by the liver. It serves as a storage facility for bilirubin, which is eventually eliminated from the body. Therefore, the gallbladder helps to keep the body clean and safe.

The fat is emulsified with the help of gallbladder-pumped bile juice, after which it is easily absorbed and used by the body.

Without bile produced by the gallbladder, some of the nutrition and good fat required for the body to function will be eliminated while urinating. So, the organ may not be mandatory but certainly performs the important task of retaining essential nutrients in our body, unlike any man-made alternative that has been discovered so far. Let's get started.

Hello dear reader!

I hope you will enjoy this book.

I want to let you know how important your purchase and your judgement can be to me.

I write for passion and I think that the arguments of this book can help people to deepen into the topic, answer some questions and get the basis of your knowledge about the argument of this book.

Writing a book is a great challenge that keeps you busy for hours on end, trying to create the best you can do.

One way that you can support my work is by leaving me a review one this book.

I can't THANK YOU enough for this.

Enough with the words now, the book is waiting for you.

Meet Our Authors: www.amzcreativelab.com

Chapter 1: Introduction to the Gallbladder

The gallbladder is a small organ located beneath the right rib cage, just below the liver. Its size varies by individual and can be as small as a plum or as large as a large apple. It is connected to the liver and sits on top of the small bowel. The gallbladder is linked to the intestines by small tubes known as bile ducts. These bile ducts are responsible for transporting the yellow/greenish fluid (bile) produced by the liver.

So, what is bile, and why is it important? Bile is a digestive fluid produced by the liver and stored in the gallbladder. Bile aids in the absorption of fats and other fat-soluble substances (think vitamins A, D, E, and K). Bile is made up of water, phospholipids, cholesterol, and other chemicals that aid digestion. But, in addition to promoting proper digestion, bile is important to our bodies because it is an important excretion 'route' for many waste products, such as bilirubin (a byproduct of red blood cells recycled by the liver).

The gallbladder expands when bile accumulates, which usually happens when a person hasn't eaten in a long time, such as when a person is sick, fasting, or dieting severely and following a fad diet. The gallbladder's primary function is to collect and store bile before releasing it into the bile ducts during food consumption. The bile is then transported to our intestine via the ducts. The bile then breaks down the ingested fat into tiny droplets that can be easily absorbed. Because bile is stored in the gallbladder, the gallbladder's importance is self-evident.

All of this appears to be normal, so how do gallstones form? When does this disruption take place? To understand how gallstones form, experts recommend visualizing the digestive organs as a 'biliary tree.' This biliary tree is made up of four organs that are linked together by tubes. To better understand this, imagine yourself drawing a diagram of your liver, gallbladder, pancreas, and small bowel. The liver is at the top of the diagram, followed by the gallbladder on the right, the pancreas on the left, and the small bowel at the bottom. All of these organs are linked together by crisscrossed pipes. Is it becoming clearer?

The purpose of the biliary tree is to transport secretions throughout the body, assisting digestion, absorbing nutrients, and eliminating waste. The cycle begins with the liver, of course, and then the secretions move to the gallbladder, then the pancreas, and finally the small bowel. The goal of this cycle is to remove waste from the body in the form of bile, a yellow/greenish fluid.

What you may not realize is that the body does not constantly eliminate bile. Instead, it stores bile and other secretions and uses them as needed. In order to support proper digestion, the body decides to store bile so that it can be used efficiently and immediately when we begin to eat.

The bile duct, which is essentially a muscle that resembles a valve, closes when there is no food in the small bowel and opens when we begin eating, allowing bile, secretions, and other important enzymes to pass through and contribute to normal digestion.

And while the bile ducts close when there is no more food in the small bowel (as when fasting), the liver and pancreas have no way of knowing, so they do not close the doors and stop working. They are constantly secreting secretions as well as bile. And because they are also unaware of our eating habits or whether we have an appetite or not, they receive no indication that they should cease production. That is why digestive secretions, including bile, are constantly pumped out, implying that there is always extra bile inside. But what happens when the bile ducts receive the message that there is no need for bile in the small bowel and close down while the liver and pancreas do not? In that case, where does the bile go? When bile is released from the gallbladder and comes into contact with a closed bile duct, it has no choice but to return to the gallbladder.

This pear-shaped organ is important for digestion because it collects and stores extra bile that cannot be transferred to the small bowel. When we begin to eat, the gallbladder contracts, squeezing out the bile that aids digestion.

Anatomy of Gallbladder

This hollow organ, which lives in the curve at the bottom of the liver, is made up of three segments: the fundus, the body, and the neck. The Hartmann's pouch is a mucosal sac that is found at the point where the neck of the gallbladder and the cystic duct meet. Multiple layers of epithelial cells (one of the body's cells) are found in the cavities of organs and as a protective, surrounding membrane around them and blood vessels, as in many other organs. A mucosal layer forms this, and the Hartmann's pouch is a mucosal pouch. Gallbladder stones are typically found in this pouch.

Symptoms of Gallbladder Problems

The symptoms below are indicators that you may have problems with the gallbladder that needs to be checked by your doctor.

Pain: The major way to know that there is a problem with the gallbladder is when you feel pain close to the mid-upper right part of your abdomen. It can either be severe and frequent or mild and intermittent. In some cases, you would begin to feel the pain move to other parts of the body like your chest and back.

Vomiting and Nausea: This symptom is common to all the different types of gallbladder problems. However, digestive problems like gas and acid reflux are peculiar to chronic gallbladder disease.

Chronic Diarrhea: If you have more than 4 bowel movements every day for at least 3 months, it is most likely an indicator that you have chronic gallbladder disease.

Fever or Chills: Unexplained fever or chills is an indicator that you may have an infection. If it is confirmed that you have an infection, it is important to begin treatment immediately before it gets worse and more dangerous. If you allow the infection to get to other parts of your body, it can become life-threatening.

Unusual Urine or Stools: Dark-colored urine or lighter-colored stools are signs that the common bile duct is blocked.

Jaundice: Jaundice or yellow-tinted skin may be a sign that there is stone or blockage in the common bile duct. The common bile duct is the medium that goes to the small intestine from the gallbladder.

Potential Gallbladder Problems

Any disease that is capable of affecting the gallbladder is known as gallbladder disease. There are two possible problems that may occur with the gallbladder and we would look at them below:

Inflammation of the Gallbladder

This is also referred to as cholecystitis and it can either be long-term (chronic) or short-term (acute). Chronic inflammation is caused by several acute cholecystitis attacks. If left untreated, this condition can cause damage to the gallbladder, making it not function correctly.

Gallstones

These are small, hard deposits that build up in the gallbladder. They can develop without being noticed for several years. It's safe to say that several people have gallstones without knowing. They end up causing problems like infection, inflammation, and pain.

Gallstones are commonly the cause of acute cholecystitis. Gallstones start out small, about a few millimeters wide, and then grow to several centimeters wide. Some people have multiple gallstones, while others have only one large gallstone. As the gallstones grow in size, they begin to clog the exit routes from the gallbladder. The majority of gallstones form from cholesterol stored in the bile of the gallbladder. Another type of gallstone is pigment stone, which is formed from calcium bilirubin, a chemical produced by the body when red blood cells are broken down.

These are hard, pebble-like pieces of material made of bilirubin or cholesterol formed in the gallbladder. Gallstones can range in size from as small as a grain of sand to as large as a golf ball. While some people have a mix of small and large stones, others may have several tiny stones or even a single large gallstone.

When these stones become lodged in the biliary tract of the bile ducts, they can cause severe pain in the right upper abdomen. This pain is known as a gallbladder attack or biliary colic. If the symptoms are not treated, they can cause serious complications. However, gallstones that do not cause blockages and are painless can occur. Silent gallstones are the name given to this type of gallstone.

Gallstones can go unnoticed. The majority of people who have gallstones have no symptoms, which is why they are referred to as silent gallstones. They do not inhibit the function of your liver, gallbladder, or pancreas, so you will not require treatment.

What exactly is the Biliary Tract? This section of the bile duct and gallbladder is in charge of digestion by secreting bile. The bile portion of the biliary tract houses the common bile duct, hepatic duct, and cystic duct. The bile duct also aids in the movement of digestive juices and waste from the pancreas and liver to the duodenum. Bile is produced by your liver and is typically composed of bile salts, cholesterol, and bilirubin. Bile is stored in the gallbladder until it is required. When you eat, your body sends a signal to the gallbladder to move bile to the duodenum to mix with the food.

Gallstones can form if your bile contains too much bilirubin, too much cholesterol, or not enough bile salts. Researchers have yet to fully explain why these changes occur. Gallstones can also form if the gallbladder does not empty completely or as frequently as it should. Gallstones are more common in certain people due to their diet and weight.

Gallstones Symptoms

If gallstones block your bile ducts, bile will build up in your gallbladder, causing a gallbladder attack known as biliary colic. A gallbladder attack can cause pain in your right upper abdomen that can last for several hours. Gallbladder attacks are most common after large meals and usually occur at night or in the evening. If you've had one gallbladder attack before, you're more likely to have another. The attack will continue until the gallstones that are blocking the bile ducts are removed. However, if the bile duct blockage persists for more than a few hours, it may result in gallstone complications. You would not have any symptoms if your gallstones did not block your bile ducts.

The Effect of Weight on Gallstones

Obesity or being overweight increases your chances of having gallstones, especially in women. Obese people have high cholesterol levels in their bile, which can lead to gallstones, according to research. Obese people are also more likely to have a large gallbladder that is not functioning properly. Some studies have also shown that people who carry their fat around their waist are more likely to develop gallstones than people who carry their fat around their thighs and hips. Rapid weight loss can increase your risk of developing gallstones.

The Influence of Rapid Weight Loss on Gallstones

When you lose weight quickly or go without eating for an extended period of time, your liver tends to release more cholesterol into the bile. A rapid weight loss would prevent the gallbladder from properly emptying itself. While weight loss surgery can help you lose weight quickly, it also puts you at risk of developing gallstones. The type of weight-loss treatment you choose will determine your chances of developing gallstones. Surgery or diets that result in rapid weight loss have a higher risk of causing gallstones than surgeries or diets that help you lose weight gradually, such as the low-calorie diet.

Several factors can increase your chances of developing gallstones after a very low-calorie diet or weight loss surgery. These elements are as follows:

- Rapid weight loss following surgery or following a very low-calorie diet

- Gallstones that were present prior to the weight loss surgery or before starting a very low-calorie diet, especially if you had symptoms from the stones.

- A significant amount of extra weight before embarking on a very low-calorie diet or undergoing weight loss surgery.

If you need to have weight loss surgery or begin a very low-calorie diet, it is critical that you consult with your doctor about ways to reduce your risk of developing gallstones. Another way to avoid gallstones after losing a lot of weight quickly, either through weight loss surgery or very low-calorie diets, is to take ursodiol.

Risk Factors

Who is most likely to develop gallstones? There are many factors that can contribute to the formation of gallstones, including the diet that people consume, their age, sex, genetics, and body composition.

Gallstones are most common among:

- Women

- People over 40

- Overweight and obese people

- Some of the common factors also include:

- Pregnancy

- Diabetes

- Sedentary lifestyle

- Losing weight quickly (for instance, after fasting)

- Family history of gallstones

- Low HDL cholesterol

- Consuming an imbalanced diet

- High triglyceride levels

- Liver disease

- Medications with estrogen, contraceptive drugs, or hormone therapy drugs

Estrogen is known to have the ability to increase the cholesterol in the bile, as well as to decrease the proper functioning of the bladder (meaning to decrease its contractions), both of which can contribute to the creation of gallstones in the gallbladder.

Another thing you should know, which may confuse some of you, is that taking drugs that help you lower cholesterol levels can actually cause cholesterol gallstones. These drugs may lower the cholesterol levels in your blood, but they may increase the cholesterol in the bile, which may set the scene for the cholesterol gallstones to appear in the gallbladder.

How to Detect Them?

Gallstones are notorious for not letting you know they are present until it is too late. That is why they are often referred to as "silent stones," as the majority of them exhibit no symptoms at all. In fact, most people who have gallstones are unaware that they have these lumps in their gallbladder. The vast majority of gallstones are discovered by chance, whether during an abdominal ultrasound, stomach surgery, or another physical examination.

Some gallstones, on the other hand, cause excruciating pain. The symptoms, of course, vary from person to person, but when a person has a 'gallstone attack,' they are usually in a lot of pain. These attacks typically occur at night.

The most painful attacks are caused by a blockage in the bile ducts caused by gallstones. A gallstone can be moved to the bile duct and completely block the valve, thereby blocking the bile's path to the small bowel. When this occurs and the gallbladder contracts, forcing the bile out, the bile has nowhere to go, causing severe pain. This is referred to as biliary colic.

Gallstone patients may experience the following symptoms:

- Sudden and severe abdominal pain that can last from 30 minutes to several hours. The pain usually begins under the ribs on the right side and can quickly spread to the shoulder blade or side. The pain can also be felt in the tummy's center.

- Tension in the intestines following meals.

Understand that the pain caused by a gallstone is constant. That is, it does not go away or subside when you change positions or go to the bathroom.

The tricky part about biliary colic is that it is uncommon. You might think this is a good thing, but many people have allowed their gallstones to cause additional complications simply because of this. After a gallstone episode, it could be months before you have another. Make sure to contact your doctor right away if such an episode occurs.

However, if you want your gallbladder checked for gallstones, you can contact your doctor and get yourself tested. While a physical examination or a review of your medical history may indicate that you have gallstones, your doctor will order the following tests to confirm:

- |The abdominal ultrasound is performed using a wand that a technician moves around the belly to display images of your organs on a video monitor. This is usually the only test required to diagnose gallstones.

- Gallbladder Scan — Even if your abdominal ultrasound reveals no signs of gallstones, your doctor may believe you have a lump inside your gallbladder due to other symptoms or risks. In such cases, doctors will usually recommend a gallbladder scan. The gallbladder scan is performed after the doctor injects a radioactive dye into a vein in one of the arms to take pictures and determine whether or not the gallbladder is functioning properly. This scan may also reveal other issues, such as clogged bile ducts.

- ERCP (Endoscopic Retrograde Cholangiopancreatogram) — This test determines whether a gallstone is present in the bile ducts that connect your liver to your gallbladder, pancreas, or small bowel. The ERCP is performed after the doctor inserts and moves a small, flexible instrument down your throat to inspect the tubes that drain your gallbladder, liver, and pancreas.

- A complete blood test, including pancreatitis and liver function tests, may reveal abnormal liver function. These tests are useful because, if there isn't a gallstone causing you pain, they will most likely reveal the source of your problems.

- Endoscopic Ultrasound (EUS) — Like the ERCP, the endoscopic ultrasound is a test that involves moving a lightweight and flexible instrument down your throat and into your stomach to examine the tubes that drain your digestive organs. The only difference between these two similar procedures is that the ERCP employs a camera to generate a video image, whereas the EUS employs high-frequency sound waves to generate images.

- Magnetic Resonance Cholangiogram (MRC) — This is a test that employs MRI or magnetic field and radio wave energy pulses to provide images of the organs and structures within the abdomen. Doctors typically perform this test before gallbladder removal or to detect other gallbladder and bile duct problems.

How to Prevent Gallbladder Disease

There are numerous things you can do to keep your gallbladder healthy and functioning properly. Here are seven secret golden rules to remember to keep your gallbladder in good working order:

Exercise for Fitness

It is critical that you move your body and engage in some form of exercise. In terms of the gallbladder, exercise is not only important but also required. It is because it aids in the prevention of obesity. The gallbladder becomes strained when a person is obese and then develops diabetes. Exercise allows the body to engage in some form of activity, which aids in the functioning and health of the gallbladder.

Regular Glycemic Control

Having your blood glucose, cholesterol, triglyceride, and uric acid levels checked on a regular basis is one of the most helpful things you can do to keep your gallbladder healthy. Lowering these levels will undoubtedly aid in the preservation of your gallbladder's vital health.

Reduce Your Salt Intake.

Although a small amount of salt will not harm your gallbladder, if you have hypertension, you should limit your salt intake. Did you know that your gallbladder is in charge of eliminating excess salt from your body? If you have high blood pressure, your gallbladder will have a more difficult time getting rid of the extra salt. The gallbladder is in charge of ridding your body of any excess salt that is higher than the blood level. You should also determine the sodium content of your diet, which you can do by reading the labels on the foods you eat. You should also avoid taking too much sodium-containing medicine.

Drink Water

Your body requires a specific or exact amount of water to function properly and remain calm. It is best to keep your body hydrated at all times. Drink at least four glasses of water or other liquids per day. Every day, you should consume at least 8–10 glasses of water. If you want to keep your gall-bladder healthy, drink plenty of water.

Don't Smoke

Smoking has an effect on the gallbladder. Heavy smokers are well aware of this. Avoid smoking at all costs if you want to maintain and keep your gallbladder healthy. It is critical to understand that nicotine is what causes organ damage, including gallbladder damage. You should avoid smoking in order to keep your gallbladder healthy.

Eating Healthy Foods and Keeping a Regular Weight Check

Eating healthy is the key to having a fit and healthy body. You should eat healthy foods to help you fight gallbladder disease and other diseases. Consuming healthy foods at least once a day will aid in the health of your gallbladder. Consume plenty of fresh fruits and vegetables while avoiding oily, junk, and processed foods.

You must keep track of your weight and ensure that you check it regularly. Your weight should be within a healthy range. Before going to bed, you can check your value and record it in a diary. You must weigh yourself daily or on a regular basis, and record the results. Avoid gaining weight because it will undoubtedly put a lot of strain on the gallbladder.

Natural Ways to Treat Gallstones

While surgery is the most common way of treating gallstones, you can also treat them with natural remedies. Pain caused by gallstones can be intense and sharp and move to your back and up to the shoulder blade. Before you decide to treat gallstones on your own, it is important to first talk with your doctor. Your doctor can help provide you with the right diagnosis. Now, let's talk about natural treatment for gallstones.

Gallbladder Cleanse

Gallbladder cleanse or flush is used to prevent gallstones from developing. It can also be used to cure existing gallstones. It is also referred to as a liver flush. If you have gallstones and do not want to undergo surgery, you can use the gallbladder cleanse to remove the gallstones. While doctors would recommend that people who have symptoms of gallstones remove the gallbladder through surgery, several people have tried this method to avoid surgery. People who have low blood sugar or living with diabetes need to be careful as this mixture can be dangerous for them.

Olive Oil and Lemon Juice

For this method, you must fast for 12 hours during the day, then begin drinking 1 Tbsp (Tbsp) of lemon juice and 4 Tbsp (Tbsp) of olive oil every 15 minutes until you have consumed the mixture 8 times.

Vegetable and Apple Juice

For this method, drink only vegetable and apple juice until 5 p.m., then drink 9 ml of lemon juice and 18 ml of olive oil at 15-minute intervals until you have consumed 8 oz of olive oil.

Squeeze the juice from four fresh lemons. For one week, drink before your first meal. You would need to drink another glass of water after drinking the juice.

Drink 4 Tbsp of lemon juice in a cup of warm water every day before your first meal. Do this every day until the gallstones have vanished.

Add a tsp of dried peppermint leaves to a pot of boiling water. Turn off the heat, cover, and set aside for 5 minutes to cool. Strain the leaves and sweeten with a little honey. Drink the mixture twice daily for the next 4 to 6 weeks while it is still warm. Drink it between meals to get the best results.

1 cucumber, 1 beetroot, and 4 carrots should be juiced. Mix everything together and drink it twice a day for the next two weeks.

Others promote bowel movement by using enemas in addition to lemon juice and olive oil. The additional water in the enemas would cause the bowels to move.

Vinegar of Apple Cider

This popular health supplement, also known as ACV, is frequently used to cleanse the body and in meals due to its numerous health benefits. When you have a gallstone attack, mix one Tbsp (Tbsp) of unfiltered, raw apple cider vinegar into a glass of apple juice and drink it. This would make the pain go away in 15 minutes.

Drink one tsp of freshly squeezed lemon juice and 2 tsp of apple cider vinegar (ACV) in a glass of warm water every morning before breakfast.

Yoga

Yoga has been claimed to help people pass gallstones naturally. According to one study on yoga, it was discovered that yoga can improve lipid profiles in diabetics. Another study looked at people with cholesterol gallstones and discovered that these people are more likely to have an abnormal lipid profile. The researchers, however, found no link between the presence of gallstones and these abnormal levels. While studies have shown that yoga can help relieve some of the symptoms of gallstones, there is no scientific evidence to support the use of yoga as a cure for gallstones. The following poses are thought to help people with gallstones:

- Asana Dhanurasana (Bow Pose)
- Yoga asana (Cobra Pose)
- Asana Pachimotasana (Seated forward bend)
- Yoga asana (Locust Pose)
- Yoga asana (Shoulder stand)

Thistle (Milk Thistle)

This herb, also known as Silybum marianum, can help treat gallbladder and liver problems. Milk thistle is thought to stimulate both organs, but researchers have yet to investigate the benefits of using milk thistle to treat gallstones. Milk thistle can be taken as a supplement or as a tonic in pill form. Remember to consult your doctor, especially if you have diabetes, a history of hormone-sensitive cancers, or are allergic to ragweed. Milk thistle is used to lower blood sugar levels in people with type 2 diabetes. It is also critical to ensure that you are not allergic to milk thistle before using it.

Artichoke

Researchers discovered that artichoke is beneficial to both the gallbladder and the liver because it aids in the production of bile. We have yet to see studies on the effectiveness of artichokes in the treatment of gallstones. Artichokes can be pickled, steamed, or grilled, and there is no harm in eating them if you can tolerate them. Before taking artichoke as a pill or supplement, consult your doctor first because it may cause a gallbladder attack if the bile duct is blocked.

Grass with Gold Coins

Lysimachiae Herba, also known as Asian Moneywort Herb, is primarily used in traditional Chinese medicine to treat gallstones. This has been linked in studies to a reduction in the formation of gallstones. It is more effective to take the gold coin grass just before beginning the gallstone cleanse because it softens the stones. The gold coin grass is available in both liquid and powder form.

Pack of Castor Oil

Some people prefer to use castor oil instead of a gallbladder cleanse to treat gallstones. Warm the pack first, then soak a clock in the oil before placing the cloth on your abdomen. A towel should be used to cover the cloth. You can add a heat source to the top, such as a heating pad or hot water bottle. Leave the castor oil pack on your stomach for about an hour.

Juice from apples

You can also use apple juice to treat gallstones by drinking it on a daily basis. This is because it is believed that apple juice can soften gallstones and help you pass them as a stool. This belief stems from a letter published in 1999 in which a woman described how she successfully passed out gallstones by drinking apple juice. Drinking a lot of fruit juice is not healthy if you have stomach ulcers, hypoglycemia, diabetes, or other conditions.

How to Survive Without a Gallbladder

Yes, you can live without a gallbladder because, while it is necessary for proper body function, it is not essential in and of itself. Those who have had a cholecystectomy, whether for chronic cholecystitis or other reasons, will have low bile deposits for a few days because they will only have what has been stored in the small intestine available until, gradually, it will begin to reach the duodenum directly from the liver, causing an excess of this liquid in the intestine. As a result, this liquid will not be sufficient for fat digestion, resulting in digestive problems if this type of food is consumed. The most common side effects are nausea, vomiting, indigestion, gas and flatulence, bloating, diarrhea, and colic. This recovery period usually lasts between 2 and 3 weeks, after which the food is gradually reintroduced into the diet and you can resume a normal life.

If there is an excess of bile in the small intestine, it will begin to move to and be absorbed by the large intestine, where an excess of bile salts may be produced, causing irritable bowel syndrome and diarrhea.

Many people wonder if the gallbladder becomes fat or thin, and the truth is that, due to fat reduction and other factors, weight loss, and in some cases, difficulty gaining weight afterward.

To summarize, following gallbladder removal surgery, it is necessary to adjust the diet and gradually incorporate some foods over days or weeks. In fact, 95% of those who have surgery return to eating normally in a short period of time.

What Can You Eat After Gallbladder Surgery or Cholecystectomy?

This is the main question and the truth is that you have to start by eliminating fat or eating very low-fat foods, for example, vegetable fats are generally better accepted after a cholecystectomy. These are the recommended foods if you do not have a gallbladder:

- Herbal teas and teas, such as green tea and chamomile tea
- Low-fat dairy products, whether milk, cheese, or yogurt
- Legumes without skin and in moderation
- Pasta
- Rice

- Toast and crackers

- Fruits such as berries, apples, pears, peaches, etc.

- Vegetables, except those that are difficult to digest and flatulent

- White or lean fish

- Lean meats

- The only fatty foods allowed: 54olive or seed oil, preferably raw or well-boiled, never fried.

Prohibited or Inadvisable Foods after a Cholecystectomy

Apart from the foods mentioned above, you must take into account the foods prohibited after a gall-bladder operation to eliminate them from the diet or, if the doctor indicates it, consume the right amounts so as not to suffer damage but take advantage of their nutrients.

- Chocolate

- Coffee

- Whole milk

- Fast food

- Refined carbohydrates

- Hydrogenated fats

- Fried and processed foods

- Fatty meats, such as sausages

- Butter

- Bluefish and shellfish

- Eggs, especially the yolk

- Hard-skinned legumes

- Spicy and sauces

- Flatulent vegetables such as cauliflower, cabbage, or artichokes

- Olives

- Very fatty nuts such as hazelnuts and walnuts

No Gall-bladder lifestyle

Most nut and seed oils, including canola, sunflower, corn, grapeseed, and soybean oil, should be avoided because they now account for about 10% of our calories. Small amounts of nut and seed oils, such as sesame, macadamia, and walnut, can be used as condiments or flavorings. Avocado oil is suitable for high-temperature cooking.

Dairy should be limited or avoided. Dairy isn't good for most people, so I recommend avoiding it, except for kefir, yogurt, ghee, grass-fed butter, and cheese if it doesn't bother you. Try goat or sheep dairy instead of cow dairy. Also, whenever possible, choose organic and grass-fed meats.

Consider meat and animal products to be a side dish, or as I call them, "condi-meat," rather than the main course. Meat should be served as a side dish, while vegetables should take center stage. Servings per meal should be no more than 4 to 6 oz. I usually make three or four vegetable side dishes at once.

Consume low-mercury fish that has been raised or harvested in a sustainable manner. If you eat fish, go for low-mercury, low-toxin options like sardines, herring, anchovies, and wild-caught salmon (all of which have high omega-3 and low mercury levels).

Avoid gluten at all costs. Wheat should only be consumed on rare occasions if you are not gluten-intolerant.

Sugar should be avoided at all costs. This includes avoiding sugar, starch, and refined carbohydrates, all of which raise insulin levels. Consider sugar in all of its forms to be a once-in-a-while treat that we consume in moderation. I advise them to think of it as a recreational drug. It's something you do once in a while for fun, but it's not something you eat every day.

Consume mostly plant-based foods. As previously stated, vegetables can take up more than half of your plate. The darker it is, the better the hue. The more expansive the range, the better. Stop eating starchy vegetables as soon as possible. Winter squashes and sweet potatoes are ideal in moderation (12 cups per day). There are insufficient potatoes! Even though French fries are the most popular vegetable in America, they do not count.

We're going easy on the fruits. This is where there could be some confusion. Only low-sugar fruits, including berries, are recommended, while vegans recommend eating all fruit. Many of my patients appear to be happier when they stick to low-glycemic fruits and indulge in the rest. Avoid oranges, melons, and other similar fruits in favor of bananas, kiwis, and watermelon. Consider dried fruit to be a candy, and use it in moderation.

Pesticides, antibiotics, hormones, and genetically modified crops should all be avoided. Furthermore, no pesticides, oils, preservatives, dyes, artificial sweeteners, or other potentially harmful ingredients are present. If you don't have an ingredient in your kitchen, you shouldn't eat it. Is anyone interested in polysorbate 60, red dye 40, and sodium stearoyl lactylate (all of which are Twinkie ingredients)?

Consume gluten-free whole grains sparingly. They can also cause autoimmunity and raise blood sugar levels. A grain and bean-free diet can help type 2 diabetics, as well as those suffering from autoimmune disease or digestive disorders, treat and even reverse their disease.

Consume beans only on occasion. Lentils are the best legume. Beans that are large and starchy should be avoided. Beans are high in fiber, protein, and minerals. However, they can cause digestive issues in some people, and the lectins and phytates in them can inhibit mineral absorption. A high-bean diet will cause blood sugar spikes if you have diabetes.

Examine your solution so that it can be tailored to your specific requirements. What works well for one person may not work well for another. This is what I mean when I say that with the right tests, anyone can eventually work with a functionally qualified nutritionist to personalize their diet even further.

Chapter 2: Fundamentals of No Gallbladder Diet

The gallstone diet is a combination of anti-inflammatory and low-fat diets. It is rich in alkaline and anti-inflammatory foods that will purge the toxins out of your body, keeping your organs healthy and free of irritations. This diet is also low in unhealthy fats that may raise your cholesterol and contribute to the growth of cholesterol lumps in your gallbladder. To make sure your gallbladder will stay safe, follow these guidelines.

The gallbladder tucked down underneath the liver is a somewhat obscure organ. This is where the liver's bile is stored and sent to the small intestine to help digestion.

Your gallbladder may be protected if you consume a diet rich in nutrient-dense meals that are properly balanced. Certain foods may help keep your gallbladder healthy, while others might increase your risk of gallstones or inflammation.

If you don't take care of your gallbladder, you may have to have it removed. Because of this, a gallbladder-friendly diet is required.

Foods Made From Plants

A well-balanced diet provides a wide range of nutrients. To maintain excellent health, one should eat a diet rich in plant-based foods.

Vitamins, minerals, and antioxidants are all found in plant-based diets. These may help in the prevention of gallbladder disease.

Vitamins and minerals that include antioxidants assist the body remove harmful free radicals from the body. Processed food intake is one of several external and internal variables contributing to the body's production of free radicals. Oxidative stress may be brought on by an increase in the number of free radicals in the body. Cell damage is a risk factor for several disorders, including cancer.

If you have problems with the gallbladder, it may be beneficial to your health to adjust your diet. Rather than going for foods that can aggravate the gallbladder disease, go for the following types of food:

- Vegetables and fruits rich in fiber

- Healthy fats like fish and nuts

- Coffee, which can help to reduce your risk of having gallstones and other gallbladder diseases

- Foods rich in calcium like dark leafy greens and low-fat dairy

- Plant-based proteins lime lentils, beans, and tofu

- Foods rich in vitamin C like berries

If there has been a gallstone detected in your gallbladder, don't worry. That does not mean that you have to remove your gallbladder or experience further complications that may interfere with your normal life. Quite the contrary, actually. Many gallstones almost never cause complications. However, for you to minimalize the risk that gallstones are known to carry to some extent, as well as to prevent the cholesterol from piling up inside your gallbladder and stop new gallstones from forming, it is of great importance that you make some great lifestyle changes.

Because the gallbladder is a digestive organ, it is easy to see how an unbalanced diet can contribute to its disease. That being said, changing your unhealthy diet is one of the most important, if not the most important, things you can do to manage your gallstones and prevent them from causing further health problems.

Roll up your sleeves because we're about to completely transform and healthify your kitchen. When you have gallstones, the following foods should be avoided:

Processed Food

Processed foods should not be banned solely because they contain unhealthy and fattening ingredients that will cause your weight to skyrocket. When it comes to gallstones, the main reason you should eliminate processed food from your diet is that it contains chemicals that 'mimic' the effects of estrogen, which contributes to the production of excess estrogen, and can slow down the breakdown of fat cells.

Sugar

Of course, sugar is not permitted. This sweet danger is not only to blame for the fact that you can no longer fit into your old jeans but also the source of a slew of other health problems. One of them is the formation of gallstones. To put it simply, sugar causes weight gain and inflammation, both of which significantly increase the risk of developing gallstones.

Meat with Fat

You don't have to go completely vegetarian to avoid the fat in the meat. Meat is a good source of protein and thus essential for proper body function. However, you must be cautious about the type of meat you consume. Sausage, lunch meat, and pork are examples of fatty meats that should not be consumed as part of a healthy gallstone diet. When it comes to red meat, it is best to limit yourself to one or two servings per week and choose only the leanest cuts. Always choose organic, grass-fed meat.

To avoid gallstone irritation, use only skinless poultry meat when cooking.

Food that is fried

Deep-fried foods should be avoided if you want to manage your gallstones and keep them asymptomatic. Cooking oils high in saturated fat (including foods high in saturated fat in general) such as vegetable shortening, animal fat, or margarine should be avoided. Cooking with partially hydrogenated fat that contains trans fats and saturated fats will aggravate gallstone pain and discomfort.

According to dairy experts, whole-fat dairy is one of the leading causes of gallstone complications. The fat content of dairy is harmful to your gallbladder. It is proinflammatory, and it not only contributes to further complications such as severe pain and discomfort, but it also aids in the formation of new gallstones. That is why it is critical not to consume whole-fat milk or conventional milk products such as cheese, ice cream, and frozen yogurt.

Foods Refined

If you have been diagnosed with gallstones, you should absolutely avoid eating refined foods. Refined ingredients found in white bread, white rice, white pasta, and other refined foods are easily converted to stored fat during digestion, which can raise cholesterol levels in the bile, cause gallstones to grow, and contribute to the formation of new stones.

Foods to Eat

Olive Oil to Keep Your Gallbladder Healthy

Olive oil is healthy for your heart and gallbladder. It is a reliable source of unsaturated fats to prompt your small organs to empty.

Vegetables and Fruits

You will need gallbladder-friendly fruits and vegetables, such as cranberries, avocadoes, grapes, beets, and berries. Oranges, bell peppers, and broccoli have vitamin C and fiber. Lack of this vitamin can increase the chances of gallstone. Moreover, pectin-rich fruits, such as citrus, strawberries, and apples, are suitable for your gallbladders. Radishes are appropriate options to increase the flow of bile. If you are suffering from gallbladder problems, avoid consuming radishes.

Poultry, Fish, and Meat

The rounds or loins have less fat; therefore, these cuts are safe for your health. Any skinless chicken, lamb, or fish are good choices for you. Protein is vital for the growth and repair of body tissues.

Dairy products and red meat offer sufficient protein to your body. Remember, they are high in fat; therefore, you have to be careful. A high-fat diet can increase stress on your gallbladder. Avoid processed foods because they have high salt. Fresh foods are healthy options because of their limited sugar.

Whole Grains

You can consume soy products, seeds, nuts, legumes, and soy milk. Moreover, healthy whole grains include brown rice, bran cereal, and oats. Prefer cereals and bread containing several grains and high fiber. Focus on the fat content of dairy food items.

Live an Active Life

Physical activity is necessary to burn fat and shed extra pounds. It will help you protect the gallbladder and boost your mood. By exercising regularly, you can decrease the chances of gallbladder disease. Feel free to start jogging, running, or walking at your convenience.

Drink Sufficient Water

No doubt, hydration is essential to manage sufficient water in your bile. Your body needs water to keep organs happy. Some people drink eight glasses of water daily as a healthy goal. Remember, this amount may vary for each person. If you are drinking less water than the actual requirements of your body, your gallbladder will be at risk. Water can keep organs empty and avoid buildup from bile. It offers protection against gallstones and several other problems. By drinking more water, you can shed extra pounds. If you drink more water, you will eat less sugar and few calories.

Consume Nuts

Some studies prove that tree nuts and peanuts can help you avoid gallstones. It is essential to restrict the consumption of nuts. Eating too many nuts may increase the fat content in your body. Nuts have healthy fat and fiber along with plant sterols. This compound can block the absorption of cholesterol in your body. Make sure to eat almost one oz of nuts 5 times per week to avoid gallstones. You can consume nuts as snacks or sprinkle them on salad, cereals, and other dishes.

Eat Plant-Based Foods

A healthy diet offers several nutrients to your body. You will get antioxidants, minerals, and vitamins from plant-based foods. It allows you to avoid gallbladder diseases. Remember, antioxidants are useful for your body to prevent toxic molecules, such as free radicals. Your body can develop free radicals because of environmental stresses and natural processes, such as processed foods. The buildup of free radicals may increase the chances of oxidative stress. It can increase the chances of cell damage that will be the reason for cancer and several other diseases.

Avoid the following ingredients for a healthy gallbladder diet:

- Vegetable Oil
- Peanut Oil
- Subtle White Foods (bread, pasta, and so forth.)
- Ingredients High In Fats
- Processed Ingredients

You must keep away from positive meals to help protect your gallbladder. The largest problematic ingredients are excessive fats and processed foods. Foods which might be greasy or fried in oils like vegetable oil and peanut oil are extra hard to cut down and can cause gallbladder troubles.

Foods with trans fats, like those in processed or commercially baked products, also can be harmful to gallbladder health.

Avoiding delicate white ingredients like white pasta, bread, and sugars can guard your gallbladder. You must also avoid alcohol and tobacco.

Some meals may also increase the possibility of developing gallbladder disorders such as gallstones.

People who have concerns about the fitness of their gallbladder need to recollect averting or limiting the following food types.

Refined carbohydrates

Carbs are a key part of the general public's weight-reduction plan, and unrefined carbohydrates, which include entire grains and oats, can offer important nutrients.

However, refined carbohydrates may additionally increase the threat of gallbladder issues. In one study, researchers discovered that ingesting 40 grams (g) or extra sugar daily doubled the danger of gallstones with signs.

Carbs to limit or avoid encompass:

- Introduced sugars and sweeteners
- White flour
- Other subtle grains
- Premade baked goods, consisting of cookies and desserts
- Candy and chocolate

The gallbladder produces bile that allows the frame to digest fat. An excessive intake of fat, specifically saturated and trans fats may pressure this process.

Researchers have discovered that those who eat red, processed meats and eggs as a part of an ordinary unhealthful weight-reduction plan have a higher risk of gallstones.

Unhealthful fat is present in:

- Purple, fatty meats
- Processed meats

- Other processed ingredients
- Whole-fats dairy products
- Fried ingredients
- Many fast foods
- Premade salad dressings and sauces
- Premade baked goods and cakes
- Chocolate and different sweets
- Ice cream

Chapter 3: Sample 30-Day Meal Plan

DAYS	BREAKFAST	LUNCH/DINNER	SNACK/DESSERT
1	Fresh Fruit Juice	Chicken and Rice	Crispy Potato Skins
2	Raspberry and Pineapple Smoothie	Baked Lemon Salmon with Zucchini	Cucumber Chips
3	Mexican Frittata	Sautéed Turkey with Cabbage	Roasted Lentil Snack Mix
4	Blueberry Smoothie	Grilled Pork and Black Bean Bowl	Vegetable Chips with Rosemary Salt
5	Healthy Buckwheat, Millet, and Amaranth Porridge with Toasted Hazelnuts	Coconut Steamed Brown Rice	Potato Chips
6	Healthy Spiced Turmeric Cassava Pancakes	Sweet Potato and Beef Curry	Mango Trail Mix
7	Pear and Mango Smoothie	Spiced Grilled Chicken with Detox Salad and Mango Salsa	Cabbage Sticks
8	Pineapple Smoothie	Tuna Casserole	Hearty Buttery Walnuts
9	Mango Ginger Smoothie	Poached Halibut in Orange Sauce	Butter and Garlic Mushrooms
10	Almond Butter and Blueberry Smoothie	Salmon Baked in Foil with Fresh Thyme	Savory Collard Chips
11	Green Apple Smoothie	Cajun Catfish	Spritz Cookies
12	Mint and Cumin Salted Lassi	Sardine Fish Cakes	Fruit Crunch
13	Kiwi Strawberry Banana Smoothie	Cod and Green Bean Risotto	Pudding Glass with Banana and Whipped Cream
14	Cassava Crepes	Lemon, Garlic, Cilantro Tuna, and Rice	Chocolate Beet Cake
15	Broccoli Frittata	Pan-Seared Chicken with Turnip Greens	Strawberry Pie

16	Amaranth Porridge	Summer Ratatouille	Chocolate Biscotti with Walnuts
17	Coconut Yogurt with Acai Berry Granola	Sea Bass with Tomatoes, Olives, and Capers	Chilled Banana Pudding
18	Greek Omelet	Chicken with Broccoli Stir-Fry	Pecans-Cinnamon Pumpkin Custards
19	Turmeric Oatmeal	Cheesy Tortilla Casserole	Pumpkin Cheesecake
20	Gluten-Free Nut Breakfast Cereal	Asparagus Quinoa and Steak Bowl	Small Chocolate Cakes
21	Detoxifying Tropical Fruit Smoothie Breakfast Bowls	Yummy Chicken and Sweet Potato Stew	Strawberry Whipped Cream Cake
22	Healthy Hot MultiGrains Bowl	Avocado-Kale Salad with Grilled Lime Steak	Strawberry Mint Yogurt
23	Healthy Brown Rice Breakfast Bowl	Tangy Fillets with Sweet Potato Flakes	Papaya and Mint Sorbet
24	Passionfruit, Raspberry, and Coconut Yoghurt Chia Parfait	Detox Salad with Grilled White Fish	Grapefruit Compote
25	Raspberry and Pineapple Smoothie	Steamed Chicken with Mushroom and Ginger	Sweet Cracker Pie Crust
26	Mexican Frittata	Brown Rice and Grilled Chicken Salad	Orange Custard Cups
27	Blueberry Smoothie	Roasted Garlic Lemon Cauliflower	Mixed Nut Chocolate Fudge
28	Pear and Mango Smoothie	Broccoli Steaks	Almond Barley Pudding
29	Pineapple Smoothie	Thai Tofu Broth	Fruit Skewers
30	Almond Butter and Blueberry Smoothie	Broccoli with Garlic Butter and Almonds	Ginger Tahini Dip with Assorted Veggies

Chapter 4: Breakfast

1. Fresh Fruit Juice

Preparation Time: 5 minutes

Cooking Time: 0 minutes

Servings: 1

Ingredients:

- 1 roughly chopped apple
- ¼ cup halved frozen grapes
- 1 cup ice shavings

Directions:

1. Add all the ingredients into the blender. Process until smooth. Pour equal portions into glasses. Serve immediately.

Nutrition:

- Calories: 112
- Protein: 1.16 g
- Potassium: 367 mg
- Sodium: 3 mg
- Fat: 0.5 g
- Carbs: 25.8 g
- Phosphorus: 17.4 mg

2. Raspberry and Pineapple Smoothie

Preparation Time: 5 minutes

Cooking Time: 15 seconds

Servings: 4

Ingredients:

- ½ cup crushed Ice
- 1 chopped small overripe banana piece
- 8 oz rinsed and drained pineapple tidbits
- ½ cup frozen raspberries

Directions:

1. Except for cashew nuts and stevia, combine the remaining ingredients in a deep microwave-safe bowl. Stir.

2. Microwave on the highest setting for about 5 to 15 seconds, then stop the cooking process before the milk bubbles out of the bowl.

3. Carefully remove the bowl from the microwave. Cool slightly for easier handling. Stir in stevia if using. Sprinkle cashew nuts.

Nutrition:

- Calories: 360
- Protein: 3.1 g
- Potassium: 749 mg
- Sodium: 4 mg
- Fat: 1 g
- Carbs: 90 g
- Phosphorus: 106.2 mg

3. Mexican Frittata

Preparation Time: 5 minutes

Cooking Time: 20 minutes

Servings: 2

Ingredients:

- 5 large eggs
- ¼ cup chopped green bell pepper
- ¼ cup chopped onions
- ½ cup almond milk

Directions:

1. Preheat the oven to 400°F. Using a large bowl, combine almond milk, eggs, onion and green bell pepper.
2. Whisk until all the ingredients are well combined. Transfer the mixture to a baking dish.
3. Bake for 20 minutes.
4. Serve.

Nutrition:

- Calories: 239.5
- Protein: 16.35 g
- Potassium: 243 mg
- Sodium: 216 mg
- Carbs: 5.3 g
- Fat: 17.0 g
- Phosphorus: 94 mg

4. Blueberry Smoothie

Preparation Time: 10 minutes

Cooking Time: 0 minutes

Servings: 2

Ingredients:

- ½ cup frozen blueberries
- 1 cup unsweetened almond milk
- 1 tbsp almond butter
- ¼ cup ice cubes
- 1 pinch salt

Directions:

1. First, in a blender, mix all the ingredients and mix until smooth.
2. Serve right away.
3. Enjoy!

Nutrition:

- Calories: 221
- Protein: 24 g
- Total Fat: 35 g
- Net Carbs: 27 g
- Dietary Fiber: 2 g
- Sugars: 4.1
- Cholesterol: 0 mg
- Sodium: 191 mg

5.   Healthy Buckwheat, Millet, and Amaranth Porridge with Toasted Hazelnuts

Preparation Time: 10 minutes

Cooking Time: 30 minutes

Servings: 4

Ingredients:

- ½ cup buckwheat groats
- ½ cup whole-grain amaranth
- ½ cup whole-grain millet
- 5 cups water
- 1 tsp kosher salt
- 1 tbsp flax seeds
- 2 cups almond milk
- 1 tsp ground cinnamon
- ⅛ tsp ground nutmeg
- 2 tbsp raw honey
- 4 tbsp toasted hazelnuts, coarsely chopped

Directions:

1. Rinse the grains and add to a pot of boiling salted water; lower heat and simmer for about 30 minutes or until the grains are cooked through.

2. Remove from the heat and stir in almond milk; divide among serving bowls, drizzle each serving with raw honey, and sprinkle with cinnamon and nutmeg. Top with toasted hazelnuts and enjoy!

Nutrition:

- Calories: 318
- Protein: 9.5 g
- Total Fat: 7.4 g
- Carbs: 55.7 g
- Dietary Fiber: 7.3 g
- Sugars: 9.3 g
- Cholesterol: 0 mg
- Sodium: 644 mg

6.   Healthy Spiced Turmeric Cassava Pancakes

Preparation Time: 10 minutes

Cooking Time: 10 minutes

Servings: 4

Ingredients:

- ¾ cup cassava flour
- ½ cup coconut milk
- 2 free-range eggs
- ¼ cup coconut oil, melted
- ½ tsp baking soda
- 1 tsp stevia
- 1 tsp ground ginger
- 1 tsp ground turmeric
- 1 tsp ground cinnamon
- ½ tsp ground black pepper
- ½ tbsp toasted coconut flakes
- 1 tbsp macadamia nut butter
- 1 tbsp melted coconut butter

Directions:

1. Mix all the dry ingredients in a large bowl. In another bowl, whisk the eggs and stir in coconut milk and coconut oil until well blended.

2. Now add to the dry ingredients and whisk to form a smooth batter.

3. Heat a tbsp of coconut oil in a medium skillet and cook in 2 spoonfuls of the batter for about 2 minutes; flip to cook the other side until golden brown. Repeat with the remaining batter. Serve topped with macadamia butter, coconut butter, and coconut flakes. Enjoy!

Nutrition:

- Calories: 314
- Total Fat: 28.1 g
- Carbs: 20.5 g
- Dietary Fiber: 3.5 g
- Sugars: 1.1 g
- Protein: 4.1 g
- Cholesterol: 87 mg
- Sodium: 228 mg

Preparation Time: 5 minutes

Cooking Time: 0 minutes

Servings: 1

Ingredients:

- 1 ripe mango, cored and chopped
- ½ mango, peeled, pitted, and chopped
- 1 cup kale, chopped
- ½ cup non-fat or low-fat plain Greek yogurt
- 2 ice cubes

Directions:

1. Add pear, mango, yogurt, kale and mango to a blender, and puree.
2. Put the ice and blend until you have a smooth texture. Serve and enjoy!

Nutrition:

- Calories: 293
- Fat: 8 g
- Carbs: 53 g
- Protein: 8 g

8. Pineapple Smoothie

Preparation Time: 5 minutes

Cooking Time: 0 minutes

Servings: 1

Ingredients:

- ½ cup fresh or drained canned pineapple
- ⅛ cup orange juice
- ¼ cup non-fat or low-fat plain yogurt
- ⅛ cup water
- 2 ice cubes, crushed

Directions:

1. Combine pineapple, orange juice, plain yogurt, water and ice cubes in a blender.
2. Cover and blend until smooth.

Nutrition:

- Calories: 99
- Fat: 0.9 g
- Carbs: 18.4 g
- Protein: 4.1 g

Preparation Time: 10 minutes

Cooking Time: 30 minutes

Servings: 2

Ingredients:

- ½ cup amaranth
- 1 ½ cups water
- ¼ cup almond milk
- 1 tsp stevia
- ¼ tsp sea salt

Directions:

1. In a pan, mix water, salt and amaranth, and bring to a boil; cover and simmer for about 30 minutes and then stir in milk and stevia.

2. Cook, stirring until the porridge is creamy. Serve right away.

Nutrition:

- Calories: 190
- Fat: 3.8 g
- Carbs: 27.7 g
- Protein: 7.3 g

10. Coconut Yogurt with Acai Berry Granola

Preparation Time: 10 minutes

Cooking Time: 0 minutes

Servings: 2

Ingredients:

- 2 cup unflavored coconut yogurt
- 2 tsp raw honey
- ½ cup granola cereal
- ½ cup frozen acai berries

Directions:

1. Pour the yogurt into a serving bowl or a glass, stir in raw honey, top with granola, and sprinkle acai berries on top.

2. Serve and enjoy!

Nutrition:

- Calories: 208
- Fat: 7 g
- Carbs: 12 g
- Protein: 1 g

Preparation Time: 5 minutes

Cooking Time: 10 minutes

Servings: 2

Ingredients:

- 3 eggs
- ½ cup parsley
- ¼ tsp salt
- ¼ tsp ground pepper
- 1 tsp olive oil
- ¼ cup spinach
- 1 plum tomato
- ½ cup non-fat or low-fat feta cheese
- 6 pitted Kalamata olives

Directions:

1. In a bowl, whisk together eggs, parsley, pepper and salt
2. In a skillet, add the egg mixture and sprinkle the remaining ingredients. Cook for 2–3 minutes per side. Serve and enjoy!

Nutrition:

- Calories: 164
- Fat: 4 g
- Carbs: 14 g
- Protein: 19 g

12.   Turmeric Oatmeal

Preparation Time: 5 minutes

Cooking Time: 5 minutes

Servings: 2

Ingredients:

- 2 cups water
- 1 tsp turmeric powder
- Mint leaves, as you like
- 1 cup whole-rolled oats
- 2 splashes oat milk

Directions:

1. Place your rolled oats in a bowl, add turmeric powder, milk and water, and stir to mix.
2. Add toppings, cover, and place in the fridge overnight. Serve in the morning.

Nutrition:

- Calories: 154
- Fat: 3.1 g
- Carbs: 29.2 g
- Protein: 5.1 g

Preparation Time: 5 minutes

Cooking Time: 25 minutes

Servings: 12

Ingredients:

- ¼ cup raw almond pieces
- ¼ cup raw walnuts pieces
- 4 cups gluten-free oats
- 1 tsp cinnamon
- 1/3 cup coconut oil, melted
- 1/3 cup raw honey
- ½ cup dried fruit (like raisins) to serve
- 1 cup almond milk, to serve

Directions:

1. Preheat the oven to 325°F.
2. In a large bowl, mix all the dry ingredients; in a small mixing dish, combine the coconut oil and honey, and add to the dry ingredients.
3. Mix until the oats are wet.
4. Place the mixture on a baking sheet and line with parchment paper.
5. Bake in the oven for about 25 minutes or until golden browned.
6. To serve, add dried fruit and then stir in almond milk. Enjoy!

Nutrition:

- Calories: 202
- Total Fat: 10.1 g
- Carbs: 27.2 g
- Dietary Fiber: 3.1 g
- Sugars: 8.3 g
- Protein: 4.1 g
- Cholesterol: 0 mg
- Sodium: 11 mg

Preparation Time: 5 minutes

Cooking Time: 0 minutes

Servings: 2

Ingredients:

- 1 cup cooked lentils cooled
- 2 cups frozen mango chunks
- 1 ½ cup orange juice
- 2 tsp chopped fresh ginger
- 2 tsp maple syrup (optional)
- Pinch ground nutmeg, plus more for garnish
- 6 ice cubes

Directions:

1. Put the lentils, mango, orange juice, ginger, maple syrup, nutmeg and ice cubes in a mixer.
2. Beat over high speed for 2 to 3 minutes until smooth. Garnish with more nutmeg if desired.

Nutrition:

- Calories: 292
- Fat: 1.4 g
- Carbs: 62.8 g
- Protein: 11.3 g

15. Almond Butter and Blueberry Smoothie

Preparation Time: 5 minutes

Cooking Time: 0 minutes

Servings: 2

Ingredients:

- 1 cup almond milk
- 1 cup blueberries
- 4 ice cubes
- 1 scoop vanilla protein powder
- 1 tbsp almond butter
- 1 tbsp chia seeds

Directions:

1. Use a blender to mix the almond butter, vanilla protein powder, chia seeds, almond milk, ice cubes, and blueberries until the consistency is smooth.

2. Serve and enjoy!

Nutrition:

- Calories: 230
- Fat: 8.1 g
- Carbs: 20 g
- Protein: 21.6 g

Preparation Time: 5 minutes

Cooking Time: 0 minutes

Servings: 2

Ingredients:

- 1 cup apple cider
- 1 small banana
- 1–2 cup kale, stems removed
- Pinch cinnamon
- 1 cup green apple cut into chunks
- 1 cup water or ice

Directions:

1. In a blender, add all the fixings and blend until smooth.
2. Serve and enjoy!

Nutrition:

- Calories: 233
- Fat: 0.5 g
- Carbs: 56.4 g
- Protein: 2 g

Preparation Time: 5 minutes

Cooking Time: 0 minutes

Servings: 2

Ingredients:

- 1 tsp cumin seeds
- ½ cup mint leaves
- 1 cup non-fat or low-fat plain yogurt, unsweetened
- ½ cup water

Directions:

1. Toast the cumin seeds in a dry skillet over medium heat for 1 to 2 minutes, until fragrant.
2. Transfer the seeds to your blender, then add the mint, yogurt and water, and process until smooth. Serve immediately.

Nutrition:

- Calories: 114
- Fat: 6 g
- Carbs: 5 g
- Protein: 10 g

18. Kiwi Strawberry Banana Smoothie

Preparation Time: 5 minutes

Cooking Time: 0 minutes

Servings: 4

Ingredients:

- 2 cups sliced fresh strawberries
- 1 small banana, sliced
- 6 oz non-fat or low-fat Greek yogurt
- 1 cup ice cubes
- ½ kiwi fruit, peeled and sliced

Directions:

1. In a mixer, mix all the ingredients. Cover and mix until smooth.
2. Serve and enjoy!

Nutrition:

- Calories: 124
- Fat: 1 g
- Carbs: 28 g
- Protein: 3 g

19. Cassava Crepes

Preparation Time: 10 minutes

Cooking Time: 15 minutes

Servings: 4

Ingredients:

- 1 1/3 cups cassava flour
- 2 egg whites
- 1 cup non-fat or low-fat milk
- 2 tsp lemon juice
- 2 tbsp non-fat or low-fat melted butter
- 1 tsp stevia
- 1 pinch salt

Directions:

1. In a mixing bowl, whisk egg whites, milk, lemon juice, butter, stevia and sea salt; gradually whisk in cassava flour until well mixed and smooth.
2. Preheat a nonstick pan and spread in about a quarter cup of batter to cover the bottom. Cook within 3 minutes per side or until golden brown.
3. Repeat with the remaining batter. Serve with a cup of tea or a glass of juice.

Nutrition:

- Calories: 227
- Fat: 7.5 g
- Carbs: 38.69 g
- Protein: 3.65 g

20. Broccoli Frittata

Preparation Time: 10 minutes

Cooking Time: 20 minutes

Servings: 2

Ingredients:

- 1 cup broccoli
- 1 tbsp olive oil
- ½ red onion
- 2 eggs
- ¼ tsp salt
- 2 oz non-fat or low-fat cheese
- 1 garlic clove
- ¼ tsp dill

Directions:

1. In your bowl, whisk eggs with salt and cheese.
2. In a frying pan, heat olive oil and pour the egg mixture. Add the remaining ingredients and mix well. Serve and enjoy!

Nutrition:

- Calories: 200
- Carbs: 9 g
- Fat: 9 g
- Protein: 14 g

Preparation Time: 10 minutes

Cooking Time: 0 minutes

Servings: 4

Ingredients:

- ¾ cup chopped fresh pineapple
- 1 medium banana, frozen
- 2 cups frozen mango, diced
- 2 cups fresh baby spinach
- ½ cup freshly squeezed lemon juice
- 1 cup coconut milk
- 2 tbsp honey
- ¼ cup unsweetened toasted coconut
- 8 tsp chia seeds
- ¼ cup chopped macadamia nuts
- 1 cup chopped fresh pineapple

Directions:

1. In a blender, blend together banana, mango, lemon juice, pineapple, spinach, coconut milk and honey until smooth.
2. Divide the mixture among serving bowls; top each serving with toasted coconut, chia seeds, toasted macadamia and diced pineapple.
3. Enjoy!

Nutrition:

- Calories: 318
- Total Fat: 16 g
- Carbs: 47 g
- Dietary Fiber: 8 g
- Sugars: 32 g
- Protein: 5 g
- Cholesterol: 0 mg
- Sodium: 27 mg

Preparation Time: 5 minutes

Cooking Time: 10 minutes

Servings: 1

Ingredients:

- 2 tbsp chopped dried apricot
- ¼ cup multigrain cereal
- 1 cup almond milk
- ¼ shredded carrot
- ¼ tsp ground cinnamon
- 1 tsp orange zest
- 1 pinch salt
- 1 pinch ground nutmeg
- 1 tbsp toasted chopped almonds
- 1 orange, sliced
- 1 tsp raw honey

Directions:

1. Combine together cereal, half of the almond milk, apricot, carrot, cinnamon, orange zest, nutmeg and salt in a saucepan; bring to a gentle boil and then stir to mix well.
2. Lower the heat and simmer for about 8 minutes.
3. To serve, stir in the remaining almond milk and serve topped with toasted almonds, orange slices and raw honey.

Nutrition:

- Calories: 285
- Total Fat: 6 g
- Carbs: 28.8 g
- Dietary Fiber: 9 g
- Sugars: 35 g
- Protein: 7 g
- Cholesterol: 0 mg
- Sodium: 306 mg

Preparation Time: 10 minutes

Cooking Time: 10 minutes

Servings: 4

Ingredients:

- 2 cups cooked brown rice
- ½ cup unsweetened almond milk
- 1 tsp liquid stevia
- 1 tbsp almond butter
- 1 apple, diced
- 2 dates, chopped
- ½ tsp cinnamon

Directions:

1. Combine almond oil, almond butter, stevia, apple and dates in a saucepan; bring to a gentle boil and then cook for about 5 minutes or until the apples are tender; stir in cinnamon and brown rice, and cook for about 5 minutes and then remove from heat.

2. Serve immediately.

Nutrition:

- Calories: 226
- Total Fat: 4.3 g
- Net Carbs: 34.4 g
- Dietary Fiber: 4.8 g
- Sugars: 8.6 g
- Protein: 5.8 g
- Cholesterol: 0 mg
- Sodium: 26 mg

24. Passionfruit, Raspberry, and Coconut Yoghurt Chia Parfait

Preparation Time: 15 minutes

Cooking Time: 0 minutes

Servings: 4

Ingredients:

- 4 tbsp organic chia seeds
- 2 cups almond milk
- ½ tsp raw honey
- ½ tsp natural vanilla extract
- 1 cup organic frozen raspberries
- ½ fresh banana
- 1/3 cup almond milk
- 1 tbsp Lucuma powder
- 1 tbsp raw honey
- 1 cup fresh passionfruit pulp
- 1 cup coconut yogurt

Directions:

1. Make the chia base by mixing milk, chia seeds, raw honey and vanilla extract until well combined; let rest for a few minutes.

2. In a blender, blend together the frozen raspberries, almond milk, banana, lucuma powder and raw honey until very smooth.

3. To assemble, divide the chia seeds base among the bottom of tall serving glasses; layer with coconut yogurt, passion fruit pulp and top with raspberry smooth. Serve garnished with fresh fruit and toasted walnuts.

Nutrition:

- Calories: 377
- Total Fat: 20.7 g
- Carbs: 27.3 g
- Dietary Fiber: 15.4 g
- Sugars: 16.9 g
- Protein: 8.1 g
- Cholesterol: 0 mg
- Sodium: 18 mg

Chapter 5: Lunch

25. Chinese Tempeh Stir Fry

Preparation Time: 5 minutes

Cooking Time: 15 minutes

Servings: 2

Ingredients:

- 2 oz sliced tempeh
- 1 cup cooked brown rice
- 1 minced garlic clove
- ½ cup green onions
- 1 tsp minced fresh ginger
- 1 tbsp coconut oil
- ½ cup corn

Directions:

1. Heat up the oil in a skillet or wok on high heat and add garlic and ginger. Sauté for 1 minute. Now add the tempeh and cook for 5–6 minutes before adding the corn for a further 10 minutes. Now add the green onions and serve over brown rice.

Nutrition:

- Calories: 304
- Protein: 10 g
- Carbs: 35 g
- Fat: 4 g
- Sodium: 91 mg
- Potassium: 121 mg
- Phosphorus: 222 mg

26. Broccoli with Garlic Butter and Almonds

Preparation Time: 10 minutes

Cooking Time: 50 minutes

Servings: 3

Ingredients:

- 1 lb fresh broccoli, cut into bite-size pieces
- ¼ cup olive oil
- ½ tbsp honey
- 1 ½ tbsp soy sauce
- ¼ tsp ground black pepper
- 2 cloves garlic, minced
- ¼ cup chopped almonds

Directions:

1. Cook the broccoli in a large pot with 1-inch of water in the bottom. Drain and arrange the broccoli on a serving platter. Heat up oil in a small skillet over medium heat. Mix in the honey, soy sauce, pepper and garlic.

2. Boil, then remove from the heat. Mix in the almonds and pour the sauce over the broccoli. Serve immediately.

Nutrition:

- Calories: 177
- Sodium: 234 mg
- Protein: 2.9 g
- Carbs: 2 g
- Fat: 6 g
- Potassium: 13 mg
- Phosphorus: 67 mg

Preparation Time: 5 minutes

Cooking Time: 15 minutes

Servings: 4

Ingredients:

- 1 cup rice noodles
- ½ sliced onion
- 6 oz drained, pressed, and cubed tofu
- ¼ cup sliced scallions
- ½ cup water
- ½ cup canned water chestnuts
- ½ cup rice milk
- 1 tbsp lime juice
- 1 tbsp coconut oil
- ½ finely sliced chili
- 1 cup snow peas

Directions:

1. Heat up the oil in a wok on high heat and then sauté the tofu until brown on each side. Add the onion and sauté for 2–3 minutes. Add the rice milk and water to the wok until bubbling.

2. Lower to medium heat and add the noodles, chili and water chestnuts. Allow to simmer for 10–15 minutes, and then add the sugar snap peas for 5 minutes. Serve with a sprinkle of scallions.

Nutrition:

- Calories: 304
- Protein: 9 g
- Carbs: 38 g
- Fat: 13 g
- Sodium: 36 mg
- Potassium: 114 mg
- Phosphorus: 101 mg

28. Broccoli Steaks

Preparation Time: 10 minutes

Cooking Time: 25 minutes

Servings: 2

Ingredients:

- 1 medium head broccoli
- 3 tbsp unsalted butter
- ¼ tsp garlic powder
- ¼ tsp onion powder
- ⅛ tsp salt
- ¼ tsp pepper

Directions:

1. Preheat the oven to 400°F. Place parchment paper on a roasting pan.
2. Trim the leaves off the broccoli and cut off the bottom of the stem. Cut the broccoli head in half. Cut each half into 1 to ¾-inch slices, leaving the core in place.
3. Cut off the smaller ends of the broccoli and save them for another recipe. There should be 4 broccoli steaks. Mix butter, garlic powder, onion powder, salt and pepper.
4. Lay the broccoli on the parchment-lined baking sheet. Using half of the butter mixture, brush onto the steaks. Put in the preheated oven within 20 minutes.
5. Remove, then flip the steaks over. Brush the steaks with the rest of the butter and roast for about 20 minutes until they are golden brown on the edges.

Nutrition:

- Calories: 86
- Sodium: 143 mg
- Protein: 0.8 g
- Carbs: 2 g
- Fat: 13 g
- Potassium: 80 mg
- Phosphorus: 61 mg

Preparation Time: 10 minutes

Cooking Time: 15 minutes

Servings: 6

Ingredients:

- 1 pizza crust
- ½ cup tomato sauce
- ¼ black pepper
- 1 cup zucchini slices
- 1 cup non-fat or low-fat mozzarella cheese
- 1 cup olives

Directions:

1. Pour and spread the tomato sauce on your pizza crust, and place the rest of the fixings on top.
2. Bake the pizza at 425°F for 12–15 minutes. When ready, remove the pizza from the oven and serve.

Nutrition:

- Calories: 320
- Carbs: 32 g
- Fat: 10 g
- Protein: 25 g

30. Sweet-and-Sour Trout with Chard

Preparation Time: 10 minutes

Cooking Time: 15 minutes

Servings: 4

Ingredients:

- 4 boneless trout fillets
- 1 tbsp extra-virgin olive oil
- 2 garlic cloves, minced
- 1 onion, chopped
- 2 bunches chard, sliced
- ¼ cup golden raisins
- 1 tbsp apple cider vinegar
- ½ cup low sodium vegetable broth
- Salt and freshly ground black pepper, as needed

Directions:

1. Preheat the oven to 375°F.
2. Season the trout with salt and pepper.
3. Heat the olive oil in your large ovenproof pan over medium-high heat. Add the onion and garlic. Sauté for 3 minutes; add the chard and sauté for another 2 minutes.
4. Add the cider vinegar, raisins and broth to the pan. Layer the trout fillets on top. Cover your pan, then put it in the preheated oven for about 10 minutes until the trout is cooked through.

Nutrition:

- Calories: 231
- Fat: 10 g
- Carbs: 13 g
- Protein: 24 g

31. Stewed Chicken with Asparagus and Carrot

Preparation Time: 10 minutes

Cooking Time: 35 minutes

Servings: 10

Ingredients:

- 2 cups zucchini, diced small
- 2 cups cooked chicken breast, cubed
- 1 cup cucumber, diced
- 2 cups tomatoes, peeled
- 2 cups carrots, shredded
- 5 cups low sodium chicken broth
- 1 cup sweet corn
- 1 cup peas
- 1 cup asparagus, diced
- Parsley for garnishing

Directions:

1. Set a large stockpot over medium heat. Add the zucchini, chicken stock, chicken, tomatoes, cucumber, carrots, corn, asparagus and peas.

2. Allow cooking for about half an hour over a medium flame, stirring continuously. Once done, place into a serving bowl and garnish with parsley.

Nutrition:

- Calories: 111
- Fat: 2.5 g
- Carbs: 13.1 g
- Protein: 10.1 g

32. Parsley Root Veg Stew

Preparation Time: 5 minutes

Cooking Time: 35–40 minutes

Servings: 4

Ingredients:

- 2 garlic cloves
- 2 cups white rice
- 1 tsp ground cumin
- 1 diced onion
- 2 cups water
- 4 peeled and diced turnips
- 1 tsp cayenne pepper
- ¼ cup chopped fresh parsley
- ½ tsp ground cinnamon
- 2 tbsp olive oil
- 1 tsp ground ginger
- 2 peeled and diced carrots

Directions:

1. Heat up oil on medium-high heat in a large pot before sautéing the onion for 4–5 minutes until soft. Put the turnips and cook for 10 minutes or until golden brown.
2. Add the garlic, cumin, ginger, cinnamon and cayenne pepper, cooking for a further 3 minutes.
3. Add the carrots and stock to the pot, and then bring to a boil.
4. Turn the heat down to medium heat, cover, and simmer for 20 minutes. Meanwhile, add the rice to a pot of water and bring it to a boil.
5. Turn down to simmer for 15 minutes. Drain and place the lid on for 5 minutes to steam.
6. Garnish the root vegetable stew with parsley to serve alongside the rice.

Nutrition:

- Calories: 210
- Protein: 4 g
- Carbs: 32 g
- Fat: 7 g

- Sodium: 67 mg
- Potassium: 181 mg
- Phosphorus: 105 mg

Preparation Time: 10 minutes

Cooking Time: 15 minutes

Servings: 5

Ingredients:

- 2 cup frozen green beans
- ½ cup red bell pepper
- 4 tsp margarine
- ¼ cup onion
- 1 tsp dried dill weed
- 1 tsp dried parsley
- ¼ tsp black pepper

Directions:

1. Cook the green beans in a large pan of boiling water until tender, then drain. While the beans are cooking, melt the margarine in a skillet and fry the other vegetables.
2. Add the beans to the sautéed vegetables. Sprinkle with freshly ground pepper and serve with meat and fish dishes.

Nutrition:

- Calories: 67
- Carbs: 8 g
- Protein: 4 g
- Fat: 5 g
- Potassium: 192 mg
- Phosphorous: 32 mg
- Sodium: 458 mg

34. Yummy Chicken and Sweet Potato Stew

Preparation Time: 15 minutes

Cooking Time: 4–8 hours

Servings: 4–6

Ingredients:

- 1-lb boneless chicken breasts, with skin, removed and cut into chunks
- 4 cloves garlic, crushed
- 1 Vidalia onion, chopped
- 1 sweet potato, peeled and cut into cubes
- 3 carrots, peeled and diced
- 3 tbsp balsamic vinegar
- 2 cups chicken broth
- 2 cups fresh baby spinach
- 2–4 tbsp tomato paste
- 2 tsp whole grain mustard
- Freshly ground pepper and salt, to taste

Directions:

1. In your slow cooker, mix all the ingredients and stir well until equally blended.
2. Cook on low for 6 to 8 hours or on high for 4–5 hours, covered.
3. Stir in the baby spinach when there are only a few minutes left in the cooking time.
4. Serve immediately.

Nutrition:

- Calories: 139
- Total Fat: 11.7 g
- Net Carbs: 2.6 g
- Dietary Fiber: 3.8 g
- Protein: 5.4 g
- Sugars: 1.2 g
- Sodium: 224 mg

35. Asparagus Quinoa and Steak Bowl

Preparation Time: 10 minutes

Cooking Time: 15 minutes

Servings: 4

Ingredients:

- 1 ½ cup white quinoa
- Olive oil cooking spray
- ¾ lb beef top sirloin steak, diced
- ½ tsp low-sodium steak seasoning
- ½ cup chopped red bell pepper
- ½ cup chopped red onion
- 1 cup frozen asparagus cuts
- 2 ½ tbsp soy sauce
- 1 avocado, sliced

Directions:

1. Follow the package instructions to cook quinoa.
2. Meantime, coat a large skillet with cooking spray and heat over medium-high heat.
3. Sprinkle the beef with the steak seasoning and cook in the skillet for about 3 minutes; add bell pepper and red onion, and cook for 3 minutes more or until beef is browned. Add asparagus and continue cooking for 4 minutes or until asparagus is heated through.
4. Stir soy sauce to the quinoa until well combined, and toss it with the beef mixture before serving with avocado.

Nutrition:

- Calories: 325
- Total Fat: 38.2 g
- Carbs: 17.4 g
- Dietary Fiber: 11.1 g
- Sugars: 6.2 g
- Protein: 26.3 g
- Cholesterol: 121 mg
- Sodium: 984 mg

Preparation Time: 15 minutes

Cooking Time: 20 minutes

Servings: 2

Ingredients:

- 1 cup organic salsa
- 2 tbsp olive oil
- ½ canned refried beans
- 1 sweet onion, diced
- ½ cup non-fat or low-fat ricotta cheese
- 3 gluten-free tortillas

Directions:

1. Warm your oven to 375°F. Coat a nonstick pan with olive oil.
2. Cook the onions in a pan over medium heat until soft; add the refried beans and cook for 5 minutes.
3. Spread a tortilla at the base of the prepared pan and spread one-third of the bean mixture, followed by the salsa and the cheese. Repeat with the remaining tortillas, beans, salsa, and cheese.
4. Bake for 15 minutes or until the cheese melts beautifully. Serve and enjoy!

Nutrition:

- Calories: 302
- Fat: 13.4 g
- Carbs: 22.1 g
- Protein: 20.1 g

37.   Chicken with Broccoli Stir-Fry

Preparation Time: 10 minutes

Cooking Time: 15 minutes

Servings: 4

Ingredients:

- 2 boneless, skinless chicken breasts, cubed
- 2 tbsp olive oil, divided
- 3 small carrots, thinly sliced
- 15 oz frozen chopped broccoli florets, thawed
- 8 oz sliced water chestnuts, drained and thoroughly rinsed
- 2 garlic cloves, minced
- 2 tsp ground ginger
- 3 tbsp balsamic vinegar, divided

Directions:

1. In a large sauté pan, add ½ tbsp olive oil and heat over medium heat. Place the cubed chicken and fried about 5 to 7 minutes until lightly browned and cooked through.
2. Transfer the chicken from the pan to your bowl with a lid and set aside.
3. Pour the olive oil, garlic and carrots into the pan, and heat over medium heat until the carrots soften, within 3 to 4 minutes.
4. Place the thawed broccoli florets, water chestnuts and balsamic vinegar into it, and cook another for 3 to 4 minutes.
5. Mix the cooked chicken with 2 tbsp balsamic vinegar and 2 tsp ground ginger, and stir until well coated. Serve over brown rice if you want, and enjoy.

Nutrition:

- Calories: 189
- Fat: 9 g
- Carbs: 12 g
- Protein: 14 g

38. Sea Bass with Tomatoes, Olives, and Capers

Preparation Time: 10 minutes

Cooking Time: 15 minutes

Servings: 4

Ingredients:

- 4 (5-oz) sea bass fillets
- 1 small onion, diced
- ½ cup low-sodium vegetable or chicken broth
- 1 cup canned diced tomatoes
- 2 cups packed spinach
- ½ cup pitted and chopped Kalamata olives
- 2 tbsp capers, drained
- 2 tbsp extra-virgin olive oil
- 1 tsp salt
- ¼ tsp freshly ground black pepper

Directions:

1. Preheat the oven to 375°F.
2. Add the olive oil to a baking dish. Put the fish fillets in the dish, flipping to coat both sides with the oil.
3. Top the fish with vegetable broth, onion, spinach, tomatoes, capers, olives, salt and pepper.
4. Cover your baking dish with aluminum foil and put it in the preheated oven. Bake within 15 minutes until the fish is cooked through.

Nutrition:

- Calories: 273
- Fat: 12 g
- Carbs: 5 g
- Protein: 35 g

39. Summer Ratatouille

Preparation Time: 10 minutes

Cooking Time: 25 minutes

Servings: 1

Ingredients:

- 1 red bell pepper, medium seeded and diced
- 1 medium red onion, peeled and diced
- 1 medium eggplant, about 1 lb, stemmed and diced
- ½ cup chopped basil
- 1 large tomato, diced
- 1 small zucchini, diced
- 4 cloves garlic, peeled and minced
- Salt and freshly ground black pepper, as needed

Directions:

1. Put the onion in a saucepan and sauté over medium heat for 10 minutes. Add water 1 tbsp at a time to keep the onions from sticking to your pan.
2. Put in the red pepper, zucchini, eggplant and garlic. Cook for 15 minutes, covered, stirring occasionally.
3. Stir in the basil and tomatoes, and season with salt and pepper. Serve and enjoy!

Nutrition:

- Calories: 64
- Fat: 0.48 g
- Carbs: 14.32 g
- Protein: 2.53 g

Preparation Time: 15 minutes

Cooking Time: 25 minutes

Servings: 4

Ingredients:

- 2 chicken breasts, boneless and skinless
- 1 tbsp dill seasoning
- ½ cup low-sodium chicken broth
- 1 bunch turnip greens, thinly sliced
- 1 chive, chopped
- 4 celery stalks, including leaves, finely chopped
- 1 tbsp allspice
- 4 cloves, minced

Directions:

1. In your small bowl, rub the seasoning all over the chicken.
2. Let the broth simmer in a large cast-iron skillet over medium heat.
3. Sauté for 5 minutes, or until the turnip greens are wilted and the onions are transparent, adding the chives, cilantro, dill allspice, cloves and nutmeg as needed.
4. Place your chicken in the center of the pan and push the vegetables to the edges of the pan to form a ring. About 7 minutes in the oven
5. Flip, cover, and cook for another 7 to 10 minutes, or until equally browned on the second side. Place the chicken on your bed of greens and top with the pan gravy.

Nutrition:

- Calories: 145
- Fat: 2 g
- Carbs: 12 g
- Protein: 22 g

41. Seared Scallops

Preparation Time: 5 minutes

Cooking Time: 6 minutes

Servings: 4

Ingredients:

- 2 tbsp olive oil, divided
- 1½ lb sea scallops
- 2 cups chopped tomato
- ½ cup chopped fresh basil
- ¼ tsp freshly ground black pepper, divided
- ⅛ tsp salt
- 1 cup fresh corn kernels
- 1 cup zucchini, diced

Directions:

1. Combine tomato, basil and ⅛ tsp black pepper in a medium bowl. Toss gently.

2. Heat a large skillet over high heat. Pour 1 tbsp of olive oil into your pan, swirling to coat. Pat the scallops dry with paper towels. Sprinkle with salt and remaining black pepper.

3. Add the scallops to your pan and cook for 2 minutes or until browned. Then turn the scallops and cook for 2 minutes more or until browned. Remove the scallops and keep warm.

4. Heat the remaining olive oil in your pan. Add corn and zucchini to the pan. Sauté within 2 minutes or until lightly browned. Add to the tomato mixture and toss gently.

5. Serve the scallops with a spinach salad, if desired.

Nutrition:

- Calories: 221
- Fat: 9 g
- Carbs: 17 g
- Protein: 20 g

Preparation Time: 10 minutes

Cooking Time: 15 minutes

Servings: 4

Ingredients:

- 2 heads cauliflower, separated into florets
- 2 tsp olive oil
- ½ tsp ground black pepper
- 1 clove garlic, minced
- ½ tsp lemon juice

Directions:

1. Warm the oven to 400°F. Bake in the preheated oven for 15 to 20 minutes. Transfer to a serving platter, then serve.

Nutrition:

- Calories: 37
- Sodium: 27 mg
- Protein: 1.8 g
- Carbs: 15 g
- Fat: 10 g
- Potassium: 272 mg
- Phosphorus: 161 mg

43. Brown Rice and Grilled Chicken Salad

Preparation Time: 10 minutes

Cooking Time: 15 minutes

Servings: 3

Ingredients:

- 10 oz grilled chicken breasts
- ¾ cup brown rice
- 1 ¼ cup coconut water
- 1 tsp minced garlic
- 2 tbsp teriyaki sauce
- 1 tbsp extra-virgin olive oil
- 2 tbsp cider vinegar
- 1 small red onion, chopped
- 5 radishes, sliced
- 1 cup broccoli, chopped
- Dash sea salt

Directions:

1. Cook the rice in coconut water following the package instructions. Take it from the heat, let it cool completely, and then fluff it with a fork.

2. Whisk together garlic, teriyaki sauce, extra-virgin olive oil and vinegar. Stir in red onion, radishes, broccoli and rice. Season with salt and stir until well blended. Serve with grilled chicken breasts.

Nutrition:

- Calories: 242
- Total Fat: 6.1 g
- Carbs: 41.8 g
- Dietary Fiber: 2.8 g
- Protein: 5.4 g
- Cholesterol: 0 mg
- Sodium: 554 mg
- Sugars: 2.9 g

44. Steamed Chicken with Mushroom and Ginger

Preparation Time: 10 minutes

Cooking Time: 10 minutes

Servings: 4

Ingredients:

- 4 x 150 g chicken breast fillets
- 2 tsp extra-virgin olive oil
- 1 ½ tbsp balsamic vinegar
- 8 cm piece ginger, cut into matchsticks
- 1 bunch broccoli
- 1 bunch carrots, diced
- 6 small dried shiitake mushrooms, chopped
- Spring onion, sliced
- Fresh coriander leaves

Directions:

1. In a bowl, combine the sliced chicken with salt, vinegar and pepper; let marinate for at least 10 minutes.

2. Move the chicken to a baking dish and top with mushrooms and ginger; bake for about 15 minutes in a preheated oven at 350°F; top with chopped broccoli and carrots and return to the oven. Cook for another 3 minutes or until chicken is tender.

3. Divide the chicken, broccoli, and carrots on serving plates and drizzle each with olive oil, and top with coriander and red onions. Enjoy!

Nutrition:

- Calories: 242
- Total Fat: 5 g
- Carbs: 10 g
- Dietary Fiber: 4 g
- Sugars: 2 g
- Protein: 37 g
- Cholesterol: 88 mg
- Sodium: 114 mg

45. Detox Salad with Grilled White Fish

Preparation Time: 10 minutes

Cooking Time: 0 minutes

Servings: 2

Ingredients:

For the Salad:

- 2 (150 g each) pre-grilled white fish
- ½ cup snap peas, sliced
- 1 cup baby spinach
- 1 cup chopped Romaine lettuce
- ½ cup avocado, sliced
- ½ cup blueberries
- 2 green onions, sliced
- ½ cup shredded carrot
- 1 large cucumber, chopped
- 1 tbsp chia seeds

For the Dressing:

- 1 clove garlic, minced
- ¼ tsp oregano
- 1 tbsp tahini
- 1 tsp honey
- 1 tbsp rice wine vinegar
- ⅛ tsp red pepper flakes
- 1 tbsp lemon juice
- ¼ tsp black pepper
- 1 tsp sesame oil
- ¼ tsp salt

Directions:

1. Combine all the salad ingredients, except the fish, in a large mixing bowl. Whisk together all the dressing ingredients in a small bowl until thoroughly combined; pour over salad and toss until well combined.

2. Enjoy the grilled white fish on top of each plate!

Nutrition:

- Calories: 256
- Total Fat: 14.1 g
- Carbs: 29.7 g
- Cholesterol: 0 mg
- Dietary Fiber: 8.5 g
- Sugars: 13.5 g
- Protein: 6.5 g
- Sodium: 343 mg

Preparation Time: 20 minutes

Cooking Time: 10 minutes

Servings: 4

Ingredients:

- 1 free-range egg
- 1 ½ cups shaved/ grated sweet potato
- ¼ cup coconut oil
- 2 tbsp Dijon mustard
- 4 white fish fillets
- Salt and black pepper, to taste

Directions:

1. Combine the egg, Dijon, salt and pepper in a shallow bowl. Put the shaved sweet potato in a separate shallow bowl. Heat the coconut oil in a heavy-bottomed pan.

2. Meanwhile, dip the fillets in the egg mix, then dredge them in the sweet potato shavings. Dip the fish a second time in the two bowls for a very crisp coating. Fry the fillets for 3–5 minutes per side or until golden and crisp.

3. Serve hot with your salad of choice.

Nutrition:

- Calories: 199
- Total Fat: 12.5 g
- Net Carbs: 8.7 g
- Dietary Fiber: 1.9 g
- Sugars: 2.2
- Protein: 16.6 g
- Cholesterol: 0 mg
- Sodium: 714.9 mg

Preparation Time: 10 minutes

Cooking Time: 0 minutes

Servings: 6

Ingredients:

For the salad:

- 1 kg lean steak
- ¼ cup freshly squeezed lime juice
- A pinch sea salt
- A pinch pepper
- 2 large carrots, grated
- 1 red bell pepper, cut into matchsticks
- 2 cups broccoli florets
- 2 cups thinly sliced red cabbage
- 2 cups kale, thinly sliced
- 1 cup walnuts
- 2 avocados, diced
- ½ cup chopped parsley
- 1 tbsp sesame seeds

For the dressing:

- ½ cup lemon juice, fresh
- 1/3 cup grapeseed oil
- 2 tsp whole-grain mustard
- 1 tbsp grated fresh ginger
- ¼ tsp sea salt
- 1 tsp raw honey

Directions:

1. Mix lime juice, pepper and salt in a small dish; sprinkle over the steak and grill for about 8 minutes on each side, or until cooked to your preference, over a prepared charcoal grill.

2. Whisk all of the dressing ingredients in a small dish until thoroughly combined; put aside.

3. Toss carrots, bell pepper, broccoli, cabbage and greens in a large mixing basin with the dressing until completely covered. Toss in the walnuts, avocado, parsley and sesame seeds to combine. Serve with the cooked steak on top and enjoy!

Nutrition:

- Calories: 332
- Total Fat: 26.6 g
- Carbs: 20.2 g
- Cholesterol: 0 mg
- Sodium: 138 mg
- Dietary Fiber: 9 g
- Sugars: 5.5 g
- Protein: 3.1 g

Preparation Time: 5 minutes

Cooking Time: 20 minutes

Servings: 4

Ingredients:

- 1 lb cod, halibut, or mahi-mahi fillets
- ½ tsp salt
- ¼ tsp freshly ground black pepper
- 1 tbsp extra-virgin olive oil
- 1 red bell pepper, cored and chopped
- 1 red onion, chopped
- 2 cups cherry tomatoes
- ¼ cup chopped pitted green olives

Directions:

1. Season the fillets with salt plus pepper.
2. In your large skillet, heat the oil over medium-high heat. Add the bell pepper and onion. Cook within 3 to 5 minutes, or until softened.
3. Add the tomatoes and olives. Stir for 1 to 2 minutes, or until the tomatoes soften.
4. Place the fillets on top of the vegetables, cover the skillet, and cook for 5 to 10 minutes until the fillets flake easily with a fork. Remove from the heat.

Nutrition:

1. Calories: 151
2. Fat: 5 g
3. Carbs: 8 g
4. Protein: 19 g

49. Artichoke and Spinach Chicken

Preparation Time: 15 minutes

Cooking Time: 5 minutes

Servings: 4

Ingredients:

- 10 oz baby spinach
- ½ tsp crushed red pepper flakes
- 14 oz chopped artichoke hearts
- 28 oz no-salt-added tomato sauce
- 2 tbsp Essential olive oil
- 4 boneless and skinless chicken breasts

Directions:

1. Heat up a pan with the oil over medium-high heat, add chicken and red pepper flakes, and cook for 5 minutes on them. Add spinach, artichokes and tomato sauce, toss, and cook for 10 minutes more, divide between plates and serve. Enjoy!

Nutrition:

- Calories: 212
- Fat: 3 g
- Carbs: 16 g
- Protein: 20 g
- Sugars: 5 g
- Sodium: 418 mg

50. Grilled Mahi-Mahi with Artichoke Caponata

Preparation Time: 15 minutes

Cooking Time: 30 minutes

Servings: 4

Ingredients:

- 2 tbsp extra-virgin olive oil
- 2 celery stalks, diced
- 1 onion, diced
- 2 garlic cloves, minced
- ½ cup cherry tomatoes, chopped
- ¼ cup white wine
- 2 tbsp white wine vinegar
- 1 can artichoke hearts, drained and chopped
- ¼ cup green olives, pitted and chopped
- 1 tbsp capers, chopped
- ¼ tsp red pepper flakes
- 2 tbsp fresh basil, chopped
- 4 (5 to 6 oz each) skinless mahi-mahi fillets
- ½ tsp kosher salt
- ¼ tsp freshly ground black pepper
- Olive oil cooking spray

Directions:

1. Warm up olive oil in a skillet over medium heat, then put the celery, onion, and sauté for 4 to 5 minutes. Add the garlic and sauté for 30 seconds. Add the tomatoes and cook within 2 to 3 minutes. Add the wine and vinegar to deglaze the pan, increasing the heat to medium-high.

2. Add the artichokes, olives, capers and red pepper flakes, and simmer, reducing the liquid by half, for about 10 minutes. Mix in the basil.

3. Season the mahi-mahi with salt and pepper. Heat a grill skillet or grill pan over medium-high heat and coat with olive oil cooking spray. Add the fish and cook within 4 to 5 minutes per side. Serve topped with the artichoke caponata.

Nutrition:

- Calories: 245
- Fat: 9 g
- Sodium: 570 mg
- Carbs: 10 g
- Protein: 28 g

51. Spicy Chicken with Minty Couscous

Preparation Time: 15 minutes

Cooking Time: 25 minutes

Servings: 2

Ingredients:

- 2 small chicken breasts, sliced
- 1 red chili pepper, finely chopped
- 1 garlic clove, crushed
- Ginger root, 2 cm long peeled and grated
- 1 tsp ground cumin
- ½ tsp turmeric
- 2 tbsp extra-virgin olive oil
- 1 pinch sea salt
- ¾ cup couscous
- Small bunch mint leaves, finely chopped
- 2 lemons, grate the rind and juice them

Directions:

1. In a large bowl, place the chicken breast slices and chopped chili pepper. Sprinkle with the crushed garlic, ginger, cumin, turmeric and a pinch of salt.

2. Add the grated rind of both lemons and the juice from 1 lemon. Pour 1 tbsp of the olive oil over the chicken and coat evenly.

3. Cover the dish with plastic and refrigerate within 1 hour. After 1 hour, coat a skillet with olive oil and fry the chicken.

4. As the chicken is cooking, pour the couscous into a bowl, pour hot water over it, and let it absorb the water (approximately 5 minutes).

5. Fluff the couscous. Add some chopped mint, the other tbsp of olive oil, and the juice from the second lemon.

6. Top the couscous with the chicken. Garnish with chopped mint.

7. Serve immediately.

Nutrition:

- Calories: 166
- Protein: 106 g
- Carbs: 52 g
- Sugars: 0.1 g
- Fat: 17 g
- Sodium: 108 mg

Preparation Time: 15 minutes

Cooking Time: 30 minutes

Servings: 6

Ingredients:

- 3 lb chicken wings (15–20)
- 1/3 cup lemon juice
- ¼ cup soy sauce
- ¼ cup vegetable oil
- 3 tbsp chili sauce
- 1 garlic clove, finely chopped
- ¼ tsp fresh ground pepper
- ¼ tsp celery seed
- Dash liquid mustard

Directions:

1. Prepare the marinade. Combine lemon juice, soy sauce, chili sauce, oil, celery seed, garlic, pepper and mustard. Stir well and set aside. Rinse and dry the chicken wings.

2. Pour the marinade over the chicken wings. Coat thoroughly. Refrigerate for 2 hours. After 2 hours. Preheat the broiler in the oven. Drain off the excess sauce.

3. Place the wings on a cookie sheet with parchment paper. Broil on each side for 10 minutes. Serve immediately.

Nutrition:

- Calories: 96
- Protein: 15 g
- Carbs: 63 g
- Fat: 15 g
- Sodium: 145 mg

Preparation Time: 15 minutes

Cooking Time: 25 minutes

Servings: 4

Ingredients:

- 10–20 chicken wings
- ½ stick margarine
- 1 bottle Durkee hot sauce
- 2 tbsp honey
- 10 shakes Tabasco sauce
- 2 tbsp cayenne pepper

Directions:

1. Warm canola oil in a deep pot. Deep-fry the wings until cooked, approximately 20 minutes. Mix the hot sauce, honey, Tabasco and cayenne pepper in a medium bowl. Mix well.

2. Place the cooked wings on paper towels. Drain the excess oil. Mix the chicken wings in the sauce until coated evenly.

Nutrition:

- Calories: 102
- Protein: 23 g
- Carbs: 55 g
- Sugars: 0.1 g
- Fat: 14 g
- Sodium: 140 mg

Preparation Time: 10 minutes

Cooking Time: 30 minutes

Servings: 4

Ingredients:

- 4 (4-oz) boneless, skinless turkey cutlets
- 3 small cloves garlic, minced
- 2 tbsp chopped fresh rosemary
- 2 tbsp chopped fresh parsley
- 1½ tsp chopped fresh sage
- ½ tsp cracked black pepper
- Grated zest 1 large lemon
- 1 cup low-sodium vegetable broth

Directions:

1. Preheat the oven to 375°F.
2. Mix the garlic, rosemary, parsley, sage and pepper in a small bowl. Rub a generous amount of the herb mixture on both sides of each cutlet.
3. Place the turkey cutlets in a 9-by 13-inch baking dish, top with lemon zest, and add the vegetable broth to the dish.
4. Cover with foil and bake for 20 to 25 minutes. Remove the foil during the last 5 minutes of baking to brown the tops of the cutlets. Remove from the oven and serve immediately.

Nutrition:

- Calories: 129
- Fat: 2 g
- Carbs: 7 g
- Protein: 19.6 g

55. Couscous with Vegetables

Preparation Time: 10 minutes

Cooking Time: 15 minutes

Servings: 5

Ingredients:

- 1 tbsp margarine
- ½ cup frozen peas
- ½ cup onion, minced
- ¼ cup mushrooms, sliced
- ½ cup couscous, uncooked
- 1 garlic clove, minced
- 2 tbsp dry white wine
- ½ tsp dried basil
- ¼ tsp black pepper
- 1 tbsp dried parsley

Directions:

1. Dissolve the margarine in a skillet over medium-high heat. Sauté the peas, onion, mushrooms, garlic and wine. Add the herbs.

2. Prepare the couscous according to the package instructions. Toss the vegetables through the hot couscous and serve.

Nutrition:

- Calories: 104
- Carbs: 18 g
- Protein: 3 g
- Fat: 2 g
- Potassium: 100 g
- Phosphorous: 52 mg
- Sodium: 160 mg

56. Fresh Kale Garlic Soup

Preparation Time: 10 minutes

Cooking Time: 25 minutes

Servings: 8

Ingredients:

- 4 tsp coconut oil
- 2 medium sweet potatoes, peeled and cubed
- 1 medium onion, finely chopped
- 2 stalk leeks, finely chopped
- 2 tsp garlic powder
- 2 cups vegetable broth
- 2 cups water
- 2 cups coconut milk
- 2 (6-oz) bags baby kale, divided
- Freshly ground black pepper, to taste
- Kosher salt, to taste

Directions:

1. In a large saucepan or Dutch oven, heat the coconut oil.
2. Sauté the sweet potato, onion, leek and garlic powder for 5 minutes.
3. Add the vegetable broth, water and coconut milk. Bring to a boil and cover, then simmer for 10 minutes.
4. Add kale, cover, and simmer for another 10 minutes.
5. Let it slightly cool, then transfer to a blender. If necessary, work in two batches to prevent hot soup from spilling into the blender during blending.
6. Season to taste and serve.

Nutrition:

- Calories: 235
- Total Fat: 17.1 g
- Cholesterol: 0 mg
- Sodium: 255 mg
- Total Carbs: 18.8 g
- Dietary Fiber: 3.7 g
- Total Sugars: 5.6 g
- Protein: 5 g

57. Creamy Chicken and Farro Soup

Preparation Time: 10 minutes

Cooking Time: 60 minutes

Servings: 6

Ingredients:

- 3 cups cooked and shredded chicken
- ¾ cup dry farro
- ¼ cup almond flour
- 4 cup chicken stock
- 1 ½ cup milk
- 1 tbsp extra-virgin olive oil
- ¼ cup unsalted butter
- 1 red onion, diced
- 2 garlic cloves, minced
- 1 large carrot, diced
- 2 celery ribs, diced
- 2 tsp minced sage
- 1 tbsp minced thyme
- Salt and pepper, to taste

Directions:

1. Heat oil in a large oil set over medium-high heat; stir in farro and toast for about 1 minute; stir in salt, pepper and stock, and then bring to a gentle boil. Lower the heat and simmer for about 20 minutes.

2. Meanwhile, melt butter in a large skillet and cook red onion, garlic, carrots, celery, salt and pepper for about 5 minutes. Stir in sage and thyme for about 1 minute, and then stir in flour for about 2 minutes; whisk in milk and simmer for about 4 minutes or until the mixture is thick; pour into the farro and stir in chicken, salt and pepper.

3. Cook for about 25 minutes or until farro is cooked through.

Nutrition:

- Calories: 410
- Total Fat: 17.1 g
- Net Carbs: 26.8 g
- Dietary Fiber: 6.4 g
- Sugars: 4.8 g
- Protein: 29 g
- Cholesterol: 79 mg
- Sodium: 658 mg

Preparation Time: 10 minutes

Cooking Time: 20 minutes

Servings: 3

Ingredients:

- 1 tbsp grated Parmesan cheese
- 4 half-ear size corn on the cob, frozen
- ½ tsp dried thyme
- ¼ tsp black pepper
- 2 tbsp olive oil

Directions:

1. In a small bowl, mix the oil, cheese, thyme and black pepper. Coat the corn in the oil mixture. Place the corn in a foil packet topped with 2 ice cubes. Place the corn on a grill and cook for approximately 20 minutes.

Nutrition:

- Calories: 125
- Carbs: 11 g
- Protein: 4 g
- Fat: 7 g
- Potassium: 164 g
- Phosphorous: 57 mg
- Sodium: 14 mg

Chapter 6: Dinner

59.   Lemon, Garlic, Cilantro Tuna and Rice

Preparation Time: 5 minutes

Cooking Time: 0 minutes

Servings: 2

Ingredients:

- ½ cup arugula
- 1 tbsp extra-virgin olive oil
- 1 cup cooked rice
- 1 tsp black pepper
- ¼ finely diced red onion
- 1 juiced lemon
- 3 oz canned tuna
- 2 tbsp Chopped fresh cilantro

Directions:

1. Mix the olive oil, pepper, cilantro and red onion in a bowl. Stir in the tuna, cover, then serve with the cooked rice and arugula!

Nutrition:

- Calories: 221
- Protein: 11 g
- Carbs: 26 g
- Fat: 7 g
- Sodium: 143 mg
- Potassium: 197 mg
- Phosphorus: 182 mg

Preparation Time: 4 minutes

Cooking Time: 40 minutes

Servings: 2

Ingredients:

- ½ cup arugula
- 1 finely diced white onion
- 4 oz cod fillet
- 1 cup white rice
- 2 lemon wedges
- 1 cup boiling water
- ¼ tsp black pepper
- 1 cup low-sodium chicken broth
- 1 tbsp extra-virgin olive oil
- ½ cup green beans

Directions:

1. Warm up oil in a large pan on medium heat. Sauté the chopped onion for 5 minutes until soft before adding in the rice and stirring for 1–2 minutes.
2. Combine the broth with boiling water. Add half of the liquid to the pan and stir. Slowly add the rest of the juice while continuously stirring for up to 20-30 minutes.
3. Stir in the green beans to the risotto. Place the fish on top of the rice, cover, and steam for 10 minutes.
4. Use your fork to break up the fish fillets and stir them into the rice. Sprinkle with freshly ground pepper to serve and a squeeze of fresh lemon. Serve with lemon wedges and the arugula.

Nutrition:

- Calories: 221
- Protein: 12 g
- Carbs: 29 g
- Fat: 8 g
- Sodium: 398 mg
- Potassium: 347 mg
- Phosphorus: 241 mg

Preparation Time: 10 minutes

Cooking Time: 30 minutes

Servings: 4

Ingredients:

- 1 red pepper, chopped
- 1 yellow onion, diced
- 1 tsp ground black pepper
- 1 tsp butter
- 1 jalapeno pepper, chopped
- ½ cup lentils
- 3 cups chicken stock
- 1 tsp salt
- 1 tbsp tomato paste
- 1 tsp chili pepper
- 3 tbsp fresh cilantro, chopped
- 8 oz cod, chopped

Directions:

1. Place butter, red pepper, onion and ground black pepper in the saucepan. Roast the vegetables for 5 minutes over medium heat.

2. Then add chopped jalapeno pepper, lentils and chili pepper. Mix up the mixture well and add chicken stock and tomato paste. Stir until homogenous. Add cod. Close the lid and cook the chili for 20 minutes over medium heat.

Nutrition:

- Calories: 187
- Fat: 2.3 g
- Carbs: 21.3 g
- Protein: 20.6 g
- Phosphorus: 50 mg
- Potassium: 281 mg
- Sodium: 43.8 mg

62. Spinach Soup

Preparation Time: 15 minutes

Cooking Time: 30 minutes

Servings: 4

Ingredients:

- 1 tbsp olive oil
- ½ sweet onion, chopped
- 2 tsp minced garlic
- 4 cups fresh spinach
- ¼ cup chopped fresh parsley
- 3 cups of water
- ¼ cup heavy (whipping) cream
- 1 tbsp freshly squeezed lemon juice
- Freshly ground black pepper

Directions:

1. Warm up olive oil in a large saucepan over medium-high heat. Put the onion plus garlic, and sauté within 3 minutes.
2. Add the spinach and parsley, and sauté for 5 minutes. Stir in the water, bring to a boil, and then reduce the heat to low. Simmer the soup for 20 minutes.
3. Cool the soup for about 5 minutes. Then, along with the heavy cream, purée the soup in batches with a food processor, a blender, or a handheld immersion blender.
4. Put the soup in the pot and warm through on low heat. Add the lemon juice, season with pepper, and stir to combine. Serve hot.

Nutrition:

- Calories: 141
- Fat: 14 g
- Sodium: 36 mg
- Carbs: 3 g
- Protein: 2 g
- Phosphorus: 50 mg
- Potassium: 300.8 mg

63. Portobello-Mushroom Cheeseburgers

Preparation Time: 15 minutes

Cooking Time: 10 minutes

Servings: 4

Ingredients:

- 4 portobello mushrooms, caps removed and brushed clean
- 1 tbsp olive oil
- ½ tsp freshly ground black pepper
- 1 tbsp red wine vinegar
- 4 slices reduced-fat Swiss cheese, sliced thin
- 4 whole-wheat 100-calorie sandwiches thins
- ½ avocado, sliced thin

Directions:

1. Heat up a skillet or grill pan over medium-high heat. Clean the mushrooms and remove the stems. Brush each cap with olive oil and sprinkle with black pepper. Place in the skillet cap-side up and cook for about 4 minutes. Flip and cook for another 4 minutes.

2. Sprinkle with the red wine vinegar and flip. Add the cheese and cook for 2 more minutes. For optimal melting, place a lid loosely over the pan. Meanwhile, toast the sandwich thins. Create your burgers by topping each with sliced avocado. Enjoy immediately.

Nutrition:

- Calories: 245
- Fat: 12 g
- Sodium: 266 mg
- Carbs: 28 g
- Protein: 14 g

Preparation Time: 15 minutes

Cooking Time: 30 minutes

Servings: 4

Ingredients:

- 3 tbsp seedless raisins
- ½ cup chopped onion
- ½ cup chopped celery
- ¼ tsp garlic, minced
- 1 bay leaf
- 1 cup apple with peel, chopped
- 2 tbsp chopped water chestnuts
- 4 large chicken breast halves, 5 oz each
- 1 tbsp olive oil
- 1 cup fat-free milk
- 1 tsp curry powder
- 2 tbsp all-purpose (plain) flour
- 1 lemon, cut into 4 wedges

Directions:

1. Set the oven to heat at 425°F. Grease a baking dish with cooking oil. Soak the raisins in warm water until they swell. Grease a heated skillet with cooking spray.

2. Add celery, garlic, onions and bay leaf. Sauté for 5 minutes. Discard the bay leaf, then toss in apples. Stir cook for 2 minutes. Drain the soaked raisin and pat them dry to remove excess water.

3. Add raisins and water chestnuts to the apple mixture. Pull apart the chicken's skin and stuff the apple raisin mixture between the skin and the chicken. Preheat olive oil in another skillet and sear the breasts for 5 minutes per side.

4. Place the chicken breasts in the baking dish and cover the dish. Bake for 15 minutes until the temperature reaches 165°F. Prepare the sauce by mixing milk, flour and curry powder in a saucepan.

5. Stir cook until the mixture thickens, about 5 minutes. Pour this sauce over the baked chicken. Bake again in the covered dish for 10 minutes. Serve.

Nutrition:

- Calories: 357
- Fat: 32.7 g
- Sodium: 277 mg
- Carbs: 17.7 g
- Protein: 31.2 g

65. Buffalo Chicken Salad Wrap

Preparation Time: 10 minutes

Cooking Time: 10 minutes

Servings: 4

Ingredients:

- 3–4 oz chicken breasts
- 2 whole chipotle peppers
- ¼ cup white wine vinegar
- ¼ cup low-calorie mayonnaise
- 2 stalks celery, diced
- 2 carrots, cut into matchsticks
- 1 small yellow onion, diced
- ½ cup thinly sliced rutabaga or another root vegetable
- 4 oz spinach, cut into strips
- 2 whole-grain tortillas (12-inch diameter)

Directions:

1. Set the oven or a grill to heat at 375°F. Bake the chicken first for 10 minutes per side. Blend the chipotle peppers with mayonnaise and wine vinegar in the blender. Dice the baked chicken into cubes or small chunks.

2. Mix the chipotle mixture with all the ingredients except tortillas and spinach. Spread 2 oz of spinach over the tortilla and scoop the stuffing on top. Wrap the tortilla and cut it in half. Serve.

Nutrition:

- Calories: 300
- Fat: 16.4 g
- Sodium: 471 mg
- Carbs: 8.7 g
- Protein: 38.5 g

Preparation Time: 20 minutes

Cooking Time: 40 minutes

Servings: 6

Ingredients:

- 2 large beef rump (sirloin) steaks
- 600 g brown or white mushrooms, sliced
- ¼ cup ghee or lard
- 2 cloves garlic, minced
- 1 medium white or brown onion, chopped
- 5 cups bone broth
- 2 tsp paprika
- 1 tbsp Dijon mustard
- Juice from 1 lemon
- 1½ cup sour cream
- ¼ cup freshly chopped parsley
- 1 tsp salt
- ¼ tsp freshly ground black pepper

Directions:

1. Lay the steaks in the freezer in a single layer for 30 to 45 minutes. Slice the steaks thinly with a sharp knife, then flavor them with salt and pepper.

2. Oiled a large, heavy bottom pan with half of the ghee and heat. Then, add the beef slices in a single layer. Do not overcrowd the pan.

3. Fry over medium-high heat until it's cooked through. Remove the slices, then set them in a bowl for later. Do the same for the remaining pieces.

4. Grease the pan with the remaining ghee. Put in the chopped onion plus minced garlic in the pan and cook until lightly browned and fragrant.

5. Put the sliced mushrooms and cook for 3 to 4 more minutes while stirring occasionally. Then add your Dijon mustard and paprika, and pour in the bone broth.

6. Add lemon juice and boil for 2 to 3 minutes, then put the browned beef slices plus sour cream. Remove from the heat. If you are using a thickener, add it to the pot and stir well. Finally, add freshly chopped parsley. Enjoy!

Nutrition:

- Calories: 300
- Fat: 16 g
- Sodium: 783 mg
- Carbs: 10.8 g
- Protein: 23 g
- Phosphorus 289 mg
- Potassium 663.4 mg

67. Herby Beef Stroganoff and Fluffy Rice

Preparation Time: 15 minutes

Cooking Time: 5 hours

Servings: 6

Ingredients:

- ½ cup onion
- 2 garlic cloves
- 9 oz flat-cut beef brisket, cut into 1" cubes
- ½ cup reduced-sodium beef stock
- 1/3 cup red wine
- ½ tsp dried oregano
- ¼ tsp freshly ground black pepper
- ½ tsp dried thyme
- ½ tsp saffron
- ½ cup almond milk (unenriched)
- ¼ cup all-purpose flour
- 1 cup water
- 2 ½ cups white rice

Directions:

1. Dice the onion, then mince the garlic cloves. Mix the beef, stock, wine, onion, garlic, oregano, pepper, thyme and saffron in your slow cooker.

2. Cover and cook on high for 4–5 hours. Combine the almond milk, flour and water. Whisk together until smooth.

3. Add the flour mixture to the slow cooker. Cook for another 15 to 25 minutes until the stroganoff is thick.

4. Cook the rice using the package instructions, leaving out the salt. Drain off the excess water. Serve the stroganoff over the rice.

Nutrition:

- Calories: 241
- Protein: 15 g
- Carbs: 29 g
- Fat: 5 g
- Sodium: 182 mg
- Potassium: 206 mg
- Phosphorus: 151 mg

68. Coconut Steamed Brown Rice

Preparation Time: 5 minutes

Cooking Time: 30 minutes

Servings: 8

Ingredients:

- 3 cups coconut milk
- 1 tsp salt
- 2 tbsp coconut oil
- 2 cups brown rice, rinsed

Directions:

1. In a saucepan, mix coconut milk, salt and oil; bring to a gentle boil; add brown rice and stir to combine well.
2. Cover and simmer for about 25 minutes or until cooking liquid is absorbed and the rice is tender.
3. Remove from the heat, stir, and serve with your favorite stew.

Nutrition:

- Calories: 260
- Total Fat: 14 g
- Net Carbs: 18.1 g
- Dietary Fiber: 11 g
- Sugar: 4 g
- Protein: 3 g
- Sodium: 291 mg
- Cholesterol: 0 mg

69. Grilled Pork and Black Bean Bowl

Preparation Time: 10 minutes

Cooking Time: 0 minutes

Servings: 6

Ingredients:

- ¾ lb grilled pork roast, diced
- 2 cups cooked black beans, drained and rinsed
- 6 cups mixed salad greens
- ¼ red onion, chopped
- ½ cup vinaigrette dressing

Directions:

1. Combine all the ingredients in a large bowl; divide among serving plates and serve right away.

Nutrition:

- Calories: 469
- Total Fat: 29 g
- Net Carbs: 48.1 g
- Dietary Fiber: 12 g
- Sugar: 19 g
- Protein: 33 g
- Sodium: 272 mg
- Cholesterol: 49 mg

70. Sautéed Turkey with Cabbage

Preparation Time: 10 minutes

Cooking Time: 20 minutes

Servings: 4

Ingredients:

- 2 turkey breasts, skinless, boneless, and sliced
- 1 head cabbage, shredded
- 2 carrots, shredded
- 3 tomatoes, pureed
- 1 cup chicken stock
- 2 tbsp olive oil
- Sea salt and freshly ground black pepper, as needed

Directions:

2. Heat the olive oil in a skillet over medium heat. Cook the turkey slices until golden brown on each side.

3. When you are almost done, add the shredded cabbage and carrots to the pan and cook, stirring, for 4–5 minutes.

4. Add the tomatoes and chicken broth, and season to taste. Stir the content well, then bring it to a boil.

5. Adjust the heat to low and simmer for 10–12 minutes to ensure the turkey is cooked through. Remove from the heat and serve hot.

Nutrition:

- Calories: 172
- Fat: 8.3 g
- Carbs: 20.9 g
- Protein: 7.9 g

71. Baked Lemon Salmon with Zucchini

Preparation Time: 10 minutes

Cooking Time: 20 minutes

Servings: 1

Ingredients:

- 1 zucchini
- 1 onion
- 1 scallion
- 1 salmon fillet
- 1 tsp lemon zest
- 1 tsp olive oil
- Lemon slices, as you like

Directions:

1. Preheat the oven to 375°F.
2. Add zucchini and onion, and sprinkle vegetables with salt and lemon zest in a baking dish. Lay the salmon fillet and season with salt, lemon zest and olive oil.
3. Bake at 375°F for 15–18 minutes, remove and serve with lemon slices.

Nutrition:

- Calories: 160
- Carbs: 1 g
- Fat: 7 g
- Protein: 22 g

72. Chicken and Rice

Preparation Time: 10 minutes

Cooking Time: 20 minutes

Servings: 4

Ingredients:

- 2 lb chicken thighs
- 1 cup rice
- 15 oz salsa
- 3 tsp salt
- 3 tbsp olive oil
- 1 ½ cup low-sodium chicken broth

Directions:

1. Cut the chicken and toss with the salt. Cook in hot oil until browned.
2. Add the rice and mix well, cooking 1 more minute to toast the rice. Add the broth and salsa, and stir.
3. Let it simmer, cover and cook within 20 minutes, Serve immediately!

Nutrition:

- Calories: 160
- Carbs: 27 g
- Fat: 3 g
- Protein: 7 g

73. Cauliflower Soup with Pancetta

Preparation Time: 15 minutes

Cooking Time: 35 minutes

Servings: 4

Ingredients:

- 4 cups chicken broth or vegetable stock
- 15 oz cauliflower
- 7 oz cream cheese
- 1 tbsp Dijon mustard
- 4 oz butter
- Salt and pepper
- 7 oz pancetta or bacon, diced
- 1 tbsp butter, for frying
- 1 tsp paprika powder or smoked chili powder
- 3 oz pecans

Directions:

1. Trim the cauliflower and cut it into smaller floret heads. The smaller the florets are, the quicker the soup will be ready.

2. Put aside a handful of the fresh cauliflower and chop it into small ¼-inch bits.

3. Sauté the finely chopped cauliflower and pancetta in butter until it is crispy. Add some nuts and paprika powder at the end. Set aside the mixture for serving.

4. Boil the cauliflower until they are soft. Add the cream cheese, mustard and butter.

5. Stir the soup well, using an immersion blender, to get to the desired consistency. The creamier the soup will become the longer you blend. Salt and pepper the soup to taste.

6. Serve the soup in bowls and top it with the fried pancetta mixture.

Nutrition:

- Calories: 112
- Protein: 10 g
- Fat: 22 g
- Net Carbs: 21 g

Preparation Time: 10 minutes

Cooking Time: 10 minutes

Servings: 4

Ingredients:

- 11 oz sardines, canned, drained
- 1/3 cup shallot, chopped
- 1 tsp chili flakes
- ½ tsp salt
- 2 tbsp wheat flour, whole grain
- 1 egg, beaten
- 1 tbsp chives, chopped
- 1 tsp olive oil
- 1 tsp butter

Directions:

1. Put the butter in your skillet and dissolve it. Add shallot and cook it until translucent. After this, transfer the shallot to the mixing bowl.

2. Add sardines, chili flakes, salt, flour, egg and chives, and mix up until smooth with the fork's help. Make the medium size cakes and place them in the skillet. Add olive oil.

3. Roast the fish cakes for 3 minutes from each side over medium heat. Dry the cooked fish cakes with a paper towel if needed and transfer them to the serving plates.

Nutrition:

- Calories: 221
- Fat: 12.2 g
- Fiber: 0.1 g
- Carbs: 5.4 g
- Protein: 21.3 g
- Phosphorus: 188.7 mg
- Potassium: 160.3 mg
- Sodium: 452.6 mg

Preparation Time: 10 minutes

Cooking Time: 10 minutes

Servings: 4

Ingredients:

- 16 oz catfish steaks (4 oz each fish steak)
- 1 tbsp Cajun spices
- 1 egg, beaten
- 1 tbsp sunflower oil

Directions:

1. Pour sunflower oil into the skillet and preheat it until shimmering. Meanwhile, dip every catfish steak in the beaten egg and coat in Cajun spices.
2. Place the fish steaks in the hot oil and roast them for 4 minutes from each side. The cooked catfish steaks should have a light brown crust.

Nutrition:

- Calories: 263
- Fat: 16.7 g
- Fiber: 0 g
- Carbs: 0.1 g
- Protein: 26.3 g
- Sodium: 776 mg
- Phosphorus: 5 mg
- Potassium: 37.9 mg

76. Salmon Baked in Foil with Fresh Thyme

Preparation Time: 10 minutes

Cooking Time: 30 minutes

Servings: 4

Ingredients:

- 4 fresh thyme sprigs
- 4 garlic cloves, peeled, roughly chopped
- 16 oz salmon fillets (4 oz each fillet)
- ½ tsp salt
- ½ tsp ground black pepper
- 4 tbsp cream
- 4 tsp butter
- ¼ tsp cumin seeds

Directions:

1. Line the baking tray with foil. Sprinkle the fish fillets with salt, ground black pepper and cumin seeds, and arrange them in the tray with oil.
2. Add thyme sprig on the top of every fillet. Then add cream, butter and garlic. Bake the fish for 30 minutes at 345°F. Serve.

Nutrition:

- Calories: 198
- Fat: 11.6 g
- Carbs: 1.8 g
- Protein: 22.4 g
- Phosphorus: 425 mg
- Potassium: 660.9 mg
- Sodium: 366 mg

Preparation Time: 10 minutes

Cooking Time: 10 minutes

Servings: 4

Ingredients:

- 1-lb halibut
- 1/3 cup butter
- 1 rosemary sprig
- ½ tsp ground black pepper
- 1 tsp salt
- 1 tsp honey
- ¼ cup orange juice
- 1 tsp cornstarch

Directions:

1. Put butter in the saucepan and melt it. Add rosemary sprig. Sprinkle the halibut with salt and ground black pepper. Put the fish in the boiling butter and poach it for 4 minutes.

2. Meanwhile, pour orange juice into the skillet. Add honey and bring the liquid to a boil. Add cornstarch and whisk until the liquid starts to be thick. Then remove it from the heat.

3. Transfer the poached halibut to the plate and cut it on 4. Place every fish serving on the serving plate and top with orange sauce.

Nutrition:

- Calories: 349
- Fat: 29.3 g
- Fiber: 0.1 g
- Carbs: 3.2 g
- Protein: 17.8 g
- Phosphorus: 154 mg
- Potassium: 388.6 mg
- Sodium: 29.3 mg

Preparation Time: 5 minutes

Cooking Time: 25 minutes

Servings: 4

Ingredients:

- 4 bone-in chicken thighs, skin removed
- 1 lb Brussels sprouts, trimmed and halved
- ½ tsp salt, divided
- ¼ tsp freshly ground black pepper
- 2 tbsp extra-virgin olive oil
- 1 onion, cut into half-moons
- 1 cup low-sodium vegetable broth
- Juice 1 lemon

Directions:

1. Preheat the oven to 350°F.
2. Season the chicken with ½ tsp of salt and pepper.
3. In your large oven-safe skillet, heat the oil over medium-high heat. Place the chicken in your skillet so that the side that had skin faces the bottom, and sear for 3 to 5 minutes, or until browned, then flip.
4. Scatter the onion plus Brussels sprouts around the chicken. Add the stock and let it simmer. Turn off the heat.
5. Transfer your skillet to the oven, then bake within 20 minutes or until cooked through. Remove from the oven.
6. Sprinkle the lemon juice over the top of the chicken and Brussels sprouts.

Nutrition:

- Calories: 275
- Fat: 12 g
- Carbs: 17 g
- Protein: 27 g

Preparation Time: 10 minutes

Cooking Time: 10 minutes

Servings: 12

Ingredients:

- 1 lb salmon, cut into cubes
- 3 eggs
- 2 tbsp whole-wheat flour
- ½ cup sesame seeds
- 4 tbsp olive oil
- 2 tbsp vinegar
- 2 garlic cloves
- 2 tsp ginger
- ½ cup scallions

Directions:

1. Mix the eggs, vinegar, scallions, 2 tbsp oil, ginger, sesame seeds and ginger. Add the salmon, then stir in the flour. Form the mixture into patties.

2. Heat the rest of the oil in a frying pan. Cook the patties for 5 minutes on each side. Serve immediately.

Nutrition:

- Calories: 130
- Carbs: 0 g
- Fat: 6 g
- Protein: 21 g

80. Artichoke Heart and Chickpea-Stuffed Portabellas

Preparation Time: 10 minutes

Cooking Time: 30 minutes

Servings: 4

Ingredients:

- 4 large portabella mushrooms, stemmed
- 1 tbsp extra-virgin olive oil
- 1 (15 oz) can low-sodium chickpeas, drained and rinsed
- 1 cup cooked brown rice
- ½ red bell pepper, cored and finely chopped
- ½ cup chopped artichoke hearts
- Salt and freshly ground black pepper, as needed

Directions:

- Preheat the oven to 350°F.
- Place the mushrooms, gill-side down, on a large baking sheet. Drizzle with the oil.
- Transfer your baking sheet to the oven, and bake for 10 minutes. Flip the mushrooms and bake for 10 minutes, or until tender. Remove, leaving the oven on.
- Combine the chickpeas, rice, bell pepper and artichoke hearts in your large bowl. Season it with salt and pepper.
- Divide the mixture among the mushrooms. Return your baking sheet to the oven, then bake for 10 more minutes or until the filling is heated. Remove from the oven and serve.

Nutrition:

- Calories: 194
- Fat: 6 g
- Carbs: 29 g
- Protein: 8 g

81.   Glazed Tempeh

Preparation Time: 5 minutes

Cooking Time: 15 minutes

Servings: 8

Ingredients:

- 2 lb tempeh, trimmed
- 2 tbsp coconut oil
- ½ cup apple cider vinegar
- 4 tbsp maple syrup
- 2 tbsp Dijon mustard

Directions:

1. Cut the tempeh into 1-inch slices. Using a medium-sized pan, heat the coconut oil until it begins to melt.

2. In the meantime, preheat the oven to 375°F and spray a baking sheet with nonstick cooking spray. Fry the tempeh for a minute on each side and place them on a baking sheet.

3. Whisk the vinegar, maple syrup and Dijon mustard in a small bowl. Generously brush the tempeh with glaze. Bake for 10 minutes.

Nutrition:

- Calories: 280
- Total Fat: 15.8 g
- Cholesterol: 0 mg
- Sodium: 56 mg
- Total Carbs: 17.7 g
- Dietary Fiber: 0.1 g
- Total Sugars: 6 g
- Protein: 21.2 g

Preparation Time: 10 minutes

Cooking Time: 5 minutes

Servings: 8

Ingredients:

- 4 cups cauliflower florets, chopped
- 1 cup grated parmesan cheese
- 6 tbsp butter
- ½ lemon, juice and zest
- Salt and pepper, to taste

Directions:

1. Boil the cauliflower in lightly salted water over high heat for 5 minutes or until the florets are tender but still firm.
2. Strain the cauliflower in a colander and add the cauliflower to a food processor
3. Add the remaining ingredients and pulse the mixture to a smooth and creamy consistency
4. Serve with protein like salmon, chicken, or meatballs.
5. It can be refrigerated for up to 3 days.

Nutrition:

- Calories: 101 kcal
- Carbs: 3.1 g
- Fat: 9.5 g
- Protein: 2.2 g

83. Roasted Lemon Chicken Sandwich

Preparation Time: 15 minutes

Cooking Time: 1 hour 30 minutes

Servings: 12

Ingredients:

- 1 kg whole chicken
- 5 tbsp butter
- 1 lemon, cut into wedges
- 1 tbsp garlic powder
- Salt and pepper, to taste
- 2 tbsp mayonnaise
- Intermittent-friendly bread

Directions:

1. Preheat the oven to 350°F.
2. Grease a deep baking dish with butter.
3. Ensure that the chicken is patted dry and that the gizzards have been removed.
4. Combine the butter, garlic powder, salt and pepper.
5. Rub the entire chicken with it, including in the cavity.
6. Place the lemon and onion inside the chicken and place the chicken in the prepared baking dish.
7. Bake for about 1½ hours, depending on the size of the chicken.
8. Baste the chicken often with the drippings. If the drippings begin to dry, add water. The chicken is done when a thermometer inserted into the thickest part of the thigh reads 165°F or when the clear juices run when the thickest part of the thigh is pierced.
9. Allow the chicken to cool before slicing.
10. To assemble the sandwich, shred some of the breast meat and mix with the mayonnaise. Place the mixture between the two bread slices.
11. To save the chicken, refrigerate for up to 5 days or freeze for up to 1 month.

Nutrition:

- Calories: 214
- Carbs: 1.6 g
- Fat: 11.8 g
- Protein: 24.4 g

Preparation Time: 15 minutes

Cooking Time: 35 minutes

Servings: 4

Ingredients:

- ½ cup Cheddar cheese, shredded
- 2 tomatoes, chopped
- 7 oz tuna filet, chopped
- 1 tsp ground coriander
- ½ tsp salt
- 1 tsp olive oil
- ½ tsp dried oregano

Directions:

1. Brush the casserole mold with olive oil. Mix up together chopped tuna fillet with dried oregano and ground coriander.
2. Place the fish in the mold and flatten well to get the layer. Then add chopped tomatoes and shredded cheese. Cover the casserole with foil and secure the edges. Bake the meal for 35 minutes at 355°F. Serve.

Nutrition:

- Calories: 260
- Fat: 21.5 g
- Carbs: 2.7 g
- Protein: 14.6 g
- Phosphorus: 153 mg
- Potassium: 311 mg
- Sodium: 600 mg

85. Spiced Grilled Chicken with Detox Salad and Mango Salsa

Preparation Time: 5 minutes

Cooking Time: 12 minutes

Servings: 8

Ingredients:

- 1 tsp extra-virgin olive oil
- 1 tbsp ground coriander
- 1 garlic clove, crushed
- 1 tsp crushed dried chili
- 1 tbsp smoked paprika
- 2 tbsp ground cumin
- 4 (159 gram each) chicken breasts, boneless, skinless
- 1 tsp red pepper flakes
- 1 tsp graham masala

For the Salad:

- 1 cup diced carrots
- 1 tbsp rapeseed oil
- 1 cup halved cherry tomatoes
- 1 cup chopped red bell peppers
- 1 cup chopped yellow bell peppers
- 1 cup chopped spinach
- 1 cup grated beets
- ¼ red onion, roughly diced
- A handful fresh parsley
- A handful fresh coriander
- A handful fresh mint
- 2 avocados, sliced

For the Mango Salsa:

- 4 cherry tomatoes, diced
- 1 mango, diced
- 1 fresh red chili, seeded and chopped
- Juice 1 lime
- Black pepper
- A handful fresh coriander, finely chopped
- Sea salt

Directions:

1. To make the marinade, combine extra-virgin olive oil, garlic, all spices and salt in a large mixing bowl. Turn the chicken in the marinade until fully coated.

2. Melt butter in a grill pan or griddle over medium heat.

3. Meanwhile, working one at a time, place the chicken breasts on the edge of a big cling film sheet and fold over to seal in the spices; gently beat the chicken with a rolling pin until flattened to approximately 1 cm thick. Cook the chicken breasts for about 6 minutes on each side on a griddle pan over medium heat, or until cooked through.

4. To make the salad, add all salad ingredients, except the avocado, to a large mixing bowl. Fold in the avocado slices gently and season with sea salt and black pepper.

Make the salsa:

5. In a separate dish, combine all the salsa ingredients; press the tomatoes with your hands until a chunky, juicy salsa forms.

6. Serve one chicken breast with a heaped spinach salad and mango salsa on the side.

Nutrition:

- Calories: 182
- Total Fat: 11.7 g
- Carbs: 8.6 g
- Dietary Fiber: 6.3 g
- Protein: 19.3 g
- Cholesterol: 65 mg
- Sodium: 76 mg

86. Sweet Potato and Beef Curry

Preparation Time: 10 minutes

Cooking Time: 6 hours 15 minutes

Servings: 8

Ingredients:

- 2 lb beef chuck steak, trimmed, diced
- 1 lb sweet potato, peeled, diced
- 1 tbsp extra-virgin olive oil
- 2 cups coconut milk
- 2 tbsp Thai red curry paste
- 1 ½ tbsp curry sauce
- 3 kaffir lime leaves
- 1 lemongrass stem, bruised
- Fresh coriander leaves
- A pinch salt and pepper

Directions:

1. Heat olive oil in a skillet set over medium-high heat and fry in beef for about 5 minutes or until browned; transfer to a slower cooker.

2. Add red onion, garlic, curry paste and lemongrass to the skillet, and cook for about 5 minutes or until fragrant; stir in coconut milk for about 2 minutes, and then transfer the mixture to the slow cooker.

3. Add curry sauce to the pot and kaffir lime leaves and sweet potatoes and stir to combine. Cover the pot and cook on low for about 6 hours or until the beef is very tender.

4. Stir the curry and remove kaffir lime leaves and lemongrass before serving. Serve topped with chopped coriander leaves.

Nutrition:

- Calories: 430
- Total Fat: 25.25 g
- Net Carbs: 15.1 g
- Dietary Fiber: 3.5 g
- Sugars: 5.7 g
- Protein: 31.9 g
- Cholesterol: 71 mg
- Sodium: 305 mg

Preparation Time: 10 minutes

Cooking Time: 20 minutes

Servings: 3

Ingredients:

- 2 cups carrots, sliced into 1-inch pieces
- ¼ cup apple juice
- 2 tbsp margarine, melted
- ¼ cup boiling water
- 1 tbsp sugar
- 1 tsp cornstarch
- ¼ tsp salt
- ¼ tsp ground ginger

Directions:

1. Cook carrots until tender. Mix sugar, cornstarch, salt, ginger, apple juice and margarine together. Pour the mixture over carrots and cook for 10 minutes until thickened. Serve.

Nutrition:

- Calories: 101
- Carbs: 14 g
- Protein: 1 g
- Fat: 2 g
- Potassium: 202 g
- Phosphorous: 26 mg
- Sodium: 65 g

88. Asparagus and Carrot Salad with Burrata

Preparation Time: 15 minutes

Cooking Time: 8 minutes

Servings: 2

Ingredients:

- 250 g white asparagus
- 250 g green asparagus
- 2 carrots
- 3 tbsp olive oil
- 1 tbsp sunflower seeds
- 1 tbsp lemon juice
- 150 g cherry tomatoes
- 1 handful arugula
- 1 spring onion
- 2 bullets burrata

Directions:

1. Peel the asparagus and cut off the lower ends. Wash the green asparagus, and the woody ends are also cut off.

2. Cut the asparagus into pieces. Clean, peel, and cut into sticks with the carrots.

3. In a saucepan, heat the oil and fry the asparagus and carrots over medium heat for 5 minutes.

4. Add the seeds to the sunflower and roast for 3 minutes.

5. Deglaze with lemon juice and add salt and pepper to season the asparagus and carrot mix.

6. Take it off the stove, then and let it cool down.

7. Wash the tomatoes and quarter them at the same time. Rocket wash and dry shake. The spring onions are cleaned, washed, and cut into pieces.

8. Mix the tomatoes, rocket, and spring onions with the asparagus, arrange them on plates and serve each with a scoop of burrata.

Nutrition:

- Calories: 671
- Protein: 34 g
- Fat: 48 g
- Carbs: 26 g
- Phosphorus: 31 mg
- Potassium: 286.6 mg

89. Quinoa Salad

Preparation Time: 15 minutes

Cooking Time: 10 minutes

Servings: 4

Ingredients:

- 200 g quinoa
- 1 mango
- 1 cucumber
- 3 tomatoes
- 1 red pepper
- 150 g lamb's lettuce
- 1 red onion
- 2 stems mint
- 150 g feta (45% fat in dry matter)
- 1 tbsp olive oil
- 1 tbsp apple cider vinegar
- Salt
- Pepper

Directions:

1. Rinse the quinoa with cold water, bring to a boil in a saucepan with twice the amount of water and cook over low heat for about 10 minutes.

2. In the meantime, peel the mango, cut it from the seed, and dice the pulp. Clean, wash and cut the cucumber, tomatoes and peppers.

3. Wash the lamb's lettuce and spin it dry. Peel and chop the onion. Wash the mint, shake dry, pluck the leaves and cut into strips. Dice the feta.

4. Drain the quinoa and transfer it to a bowl. Add the mango, cucumber, tomatoes, bell pepper, lamb's lettuce, onion, mint and feta, and mix.

5. Season the salad with olive oil, apple cider vinegar, salt and pepper.

6. Serve.

Nutrition:

- Calories: 409
- Protein: 15 g
- Fat: 16 g
- Carbs: 50 g
- Phosphorus: 347 mg
- Potassium: 321.3 mg
- Sodium: 331.9 mg

90. Zucchini Noodles

Preparation Time: 10 minutes

Cooking Time: 15 minutes

Servings: 2

Ingredients:

- 2 zucchini, peeled
- Marinara sauce of your choice
- Any other seasonings you wish to use

Directions:

1. Peel and spiralize your zucchini into noodles.
2. Add some of your favorite sauce to the Instant Pot, hit "Sauté" and "Adjust" so it's on the "More" or "High" setting.
3. Once the sauce is bubbling, add the noodles to the pot, toss them in the sauce, and allow them to heat up and soften for a few minutes, about 2–5 minutes.
4. Serve in bowls and top with some grated parmesan, if desired.
5. Enjoy!

Nutrition:

- Calories: 86
- Total Fat: 2 g
- Saturated Fat: 0.5 g
- Cholesterol: 1 mg
- Sodium: 276 mg
- Total Carbs: 15.2 g
- Dietary Fiber: 3.8 g
- Total Sugars: 8.9 g
- Protein: 3.5 g

91.   Buffalo Chicken Dip

Preparation Time: 10 minutes

Cooking Time: 7 minutes

Servings: 4

Ingredients:

- 4 oz cream cheese
- ½ cup bottled roasted red peppers
- 1 cup reduced-fat sour cream
- 4 tsp hot pepper sauce
- 2 cups cooked, shredded chicken

Directions:

1. Blend ½ cup of drained red peppers in a food processor until smooth. Now evenly mix cream cheese, sour cream and 2 tbsp Tabasco sauce with the bowl's peppers.
2. Toss in chicken and hot sauce then transfers the mixture to the Instant Pot. Cook on high for 7 minutes. Serve.

Nutrition:

- Calories: 73
- Fat: 5 g
- Sodium: 66 mg
- Carbs: 2 g
- Protein: 5 g
- Potassium: 161 mg
- Phosphorus: 236 mg

Preparation Time: 10 minutes

Cooking Time: 0 minutes

Servings: 6–8

Ingredients:

- 1 (15 oz) can black beans, drained, with liquid reserved
- ½ (7 oz) can chipotle peppers in adobo sauce
- ¼ cup non-fat or low-fat plain Greek yogurt
- Freshly ground black pepper, as needed

Directions:

1. Combine beans, peppers and yogurt in a food processor or blender, and process until smooth. Add some of the bean liquid, 1 tbsp at a time, for a thinner consistency.
2. Season it with black pepper, and serve.

Nutrition:

- Calories: 70
- Fat: 1 g
- Carbs: 11 g
- Protein: 5 g

93.   Crispy Potato Skins

Preparation Time: 5 minutes

Cooking Time: 19 minutes

Servings: 2

Ingredients:

- 2 russet potatoes
- Cooking spray
- 1 tsp dried rosemary
- ⅛ tsp freshly ground black pepper

Directions:

1. Preheat the oven to 375°F.
2. Wash your potatoes and pierce them several times with a fork. Place on a plate. Cook on full power in the microwave for 5 minutes.
3. Turn over, and continue to cook for 3 to 4 minutes more, or until soft.
4. Carefully cut the potatoes in half and scoop out the pulp, leaving about ⅛ inch of potato flesh attached to the skin. Save the pulp for another use.
5. Spray the inside of each potato with cooking spray. Press in the rosemary and pepper.
6. Place the skins on a baking sheet and bake in the preheated oven for 5 to 10 minutes until slightly browned and crispy. Serve immediately.

Nutrition:

- Calories: 114
- Fat: 0 g
- Carbs: 27 g
- Protein: 3 g

94. Hearty Buttery Walnuts

Preparation Time: 10 minutes

Cooking Time: 0 minutes

Servings: 4

Ingredients:

- 4 walnut halves
- ½ tbsp almond butter

Directions:

1. Spread butter over 2 walnut halves. Top with other halves. Serve and enjoy!

Nutrition:

- Calories: 90
- Fat: 10 g
- Carbs: 0 g
- Protein: 1 g
- Sodium: 1 mg

95. Sour Cream and Onion Dip Carrot Sticks

Preparation Time: 5 minutes

Cooking Time: 0 minutes

Servings: 2

Ingredients:

- 1 sweet onion, peeled and minced
- ½ cup sour cream
- 2 tbsp low-fat mayonnaise
- 4 stalks celery, cut into 3-inch lengths
- 2 cups carrot sticks

Directions:

1. In a bowl, whisk well sour cream and mayonnaise until thoroughly combined.
2. Stir in onion and mix well.
3. Let it sit for an hour in the fridge and serve with carrot and celery sticks on the side.

Nutrition:

- Calories: 60
- Protein: 1.6 g
- Carbs: 7.2 g
- Fat: 3.1 g
- Saturated Fat: 1.7 g
- Sodium: 38 mg

Preparation Time: 15 minutes

Cooking Time: 0 minutes

Servings: 6

Ingredients:

- 3 small-medium beets
- 3 scallions, sliced
- 2 medium carrots, shredded
- ¼ cup chopped fresh cilantro
- 2 cloves garlic
- Juice 2 fresh limes
- 1 tsp olive oil
- ½ tsp salt-free chili seasoning
- ¼ tsp freshly ground black pepper

Directions:

1. Trim and peel the beets, then shred. Place into a mixing bowl. Add the scallions, carrots, cilantro and garlic, and stir well to combine.
2. Mix the lime juice, olive oil, chili seasoning and black pepper in a small bowl. Pour dressing over the salad, then serve immediately.

Nutrition:

- Calories: 38
- Fat: 1 g
- Protein: 1 g
- Sodium: 46 mg
- Fiber: 2 g
- Carbs: 7 g
- Sugar: 4 g

Preparation Time: 10 minutes

Cooking Time: 20 minutes

Servings: 4

Ingredients:

- 2 tbsp olive oil
- 1 lb small button mushrooms
- 2 tbsp butter
- 2 tsp minced garlic
- ½ tsp fresh thyme

Directions:

1. Start by preheating the Instant pot on Sauté mode. Add olive oil and mushrooms to the pool, and sauté for 5 minutes.

2. Add garlic, thyme and butter, then mix well to coat. Seal the pot's lid and cook for 15 minutes on Manual mode with high pressure. Serve.

Nutrition:

- Calories: 118
- Fats: 7 g
- Sodium: 166 mg
- Carbs: 12 g
- Protein: 2 g
- Potassium: 395.1 mg
- Phosphorus: 98 mg

98. Savory Collard Chips

Preparation Time: 5 minutes

Cooking Time: 20 minutes

Servings: 4

Ingredients:

- 1 bunch collard greens
- 1 tsp extra-virgin olive oil
- Juice ½ lemon
- ½ tsp garlic powder
- ¼ tsp freshly ground black pepper

Directions:

1. Preheat the oven to 350°F. Line a baking sheet with parchment paper. Cut the collards into 2-by-2-inch squares and pat dry with paper towels.

2. Toss greens with olive oil, lemon juice, garlic powder and pepper in a large bowl. Put the dressing into the gardens, then massage using your hands until evenly coated.

3. Arrange the collards in a single layer on the baking sheet, and cook for 8 minutes. Flip and cook again within 8 minutes until crisp. Remove from the oven and let it cool.

Nutrition:

- Calories: 24
- Fat: 1 g
- Carbs: 3 g
- Protein: 1 g
- Phosphorus: 6 mg
- Potassium: 72 mg
- Sodium: 8 mg

Preparation Time: 10 minutes

Cooking Time: 20 minutes

Servings: 2

Ingredients:

- 1 lb cucumber
- 1 tsp salt
- 1 tbsp olive oil

Directions:

1. Preheat the oven to 425°F.

2. In a bowl, toss everything with olive oil and salt.

3. Spread everything onto a prepared baking sheet. Bake for 8–10 minutes or until crisp. Serve and enjoy!

Nutrition:

- Calories: 45
- Fat: 2 g
- Carbs: 8 g
- Protein: 1 g

Preparation Time: 5 minutes

Cooking Time: 25 minutes

Servings: 4

Ingredients:

- 1 cup dried red lentils
- 1 cup whole unsalted shelled pistachios
- ½ cup unsalted shelled sunflower seeds
- ½ cup dried cherries

Directions:

1. Cover the lentils with water in your bowl, soak for 1 hour, and drain them well.
2. Warm the oven to 350°F. Transfer the lentils to a clean kitchen towel and dab gently. Set aside for about 10 minutes to dry.
3. Spread the lentils out on a large baking sheet.
4. Transfer your baking sheet to the oven, and bake, stirring once or twice, for 20 to 25 minutes, or until the lentils are crisp.
5. Remove from the oven. Let it cool to room temperature. Transfer to a large bowl.
6. Add the pistachios, sunflower seeds and cherries. Toss to combine. Let it cool and serve.

Nutrition:

- Calories: 125
- Fat: 6 g
- Carbs: 16 g
- Protein: 3 g

101. Vegetable Chips with Rosemary Salt

Preparation Time: 15 minutes

Cooking Time: 50 minutes

Servings: 4

Ingredients:

- Olive oil cooking spray
- 2 medium beets, peeled and sliced
- 1 medium zucchini, sliced
- 1 medium sweet potato, sliced
- 1 small rutabaga, peeled and sliced
- ½ tsp salt, plus more to sweat the vegetables
- ¼ tsp dried rosemary

Directions:

1. Preheat the oven to 300°F. Spray a baking sheet with cooking spray. Line a plate with paper towels.

2. Lay the beets, zucchini, sweet potato and rutabaga in a single layer on a paper towel. Lightly salt and let it sit for 10 minutes.

3. Cover the vegetables with another paper towel and blot away any moisture on top. Arrange the vegetables on your prepared baking sheet, and spray with cooking spray.

4. Transfer the baking sheet to the oven, and cook for 30 to 40 minutes, or until the vegetables have browned.

5. Flip the vegetables and cook for 10 minutes, or until crisp. Remove from the oven. Transfer to the prepared plate to drain any excess oil.

6. In your small bowl, mix the salt and rosemary. Lightly season the chips with rosemary salt.

Nutrition:

- Calories: 72
- Fat: 0 g
- Carbs: 16 g
- Protein: 2 g

102. Ginger Tahini Dip with Assorted Veggies

Preparation Time: 10 minutes

Cooking Time: 0 minutes

Servings: 8

Ingredients:

- ½ cup tahini
- 1 tsp grated garlic
- 2 tsp ground turmeric
- 1 tbsp grated fresh ginger
- ¼ cup apple cider vinegar
- ¼ cup water
- ½ tsp salt
- Assorted veggie sticks, as you like

Directions:

1. Whisk tahini, turmeric, ginger, water, vinegar, garlic and salt in a bowl until mixed well.
2. Serve with assorted veggie sticks.

Nutrition:

- Calories: 92
- Fat: 8 g
- Carbs: 4 g
- Protein: 3 g

Preparation Time: 5 minutes

Cooking Time: 8–10 minutes

Servings: 2

Ingredients:

- 1 lb potatoes
- 2 tbsp olive oil
- 1 tbsp salt

Directions:

1. Preheat the oven to 425°F.

2. In a bowl, toss everything with olive oil and seasoning.

3. Spread everything onto a prepared baking sheet. Bake for 8–10 minutes or until crisp. Serve and enjoy!

Nutrition:

- Calories: 150
- Carbs: 16 g
- Fat: 9 g
- Protein: 2 g

Preparation Time: 5 minutes

Cooking Time: 0 minutes

Servings: 1

Ingredients:

- 2 tbsp chopped toasted cashews
- 2 tbsp chopped toasted Brazil nuts
- 2 tbsp toasted peanuts
- ¼ cup dried mango
- 2 tbsp toasted coconut flakes
- 1 tsp cinnamon
- 1 tsp cumin

Directions:

1. Mix all the fixings in your large bowl until well combined.
2. Serve and enjoy!

Nutrition:

- Calories: 110
- Fat: 2 g
- Carbs: 24 g
- Protein: 1 g

Preparation Time: 10 minutes

Cooking Time: 30 minutes

Servings: 4

Ingredients:

- 1 lb cabbage, leaves separated and cut into thick strips
- 1 tbsp olive oil
- 1 tbsp balsamic vinegar
- 1 tsp ginger, grated
- 1 tsp hot paprika
- A pinch salt and black pepper

Directions:

1. Spread the cabbage strips on a baking sheet lined with parchment paper, add the oil, the vinegar, and the other ingredients; toss and cook at 400°F for 30 minutes.
2. Divide the cabbage strips into bowls and serve as a snack.

Nutrition:

- Calories: 300
- Fat: 4 g
- Fiber: 7 g
- Carbs: 18 g
- Protein: 6 g

Preparation Time: 10 minutes

Cooking Time: 10 minutes

Servings: 8

Ingredients:

- 1 red bell pepper
- 1 can chickpeas, drained
- Juice 1 lemon
- 2 tbsp tahini
- 2 garlic cloves
- 2 tbsp extra-virgin olive oil

Directions:

1. Move the rack of the oven to the highest position. Heat the broiler to high. Core the pepper and cut it into three or four large pieces. Arrange them on a baking sheet, skin-side up.

2. Broil the peppers for 5 to 10 minutes, until the skins are charred. Remove from the oven, then transfer the peppers to a small bowl. Cover with plastic wrap and let them steam for 10 to 15 minutes, until cool enough to handle.

3. Peel the burnt skin off the peppers and place the peppers in a blender. Add the chickpeas, lemon juice, tahini, garlic and olive oil. Wait until smooth, then add up to 1 tbsp of water to adjust consistency as desired.

Nutrition:

- Calories: 103
- Fat: 6 g
- Carbs: 10 g
- Protein: 3 g
- Phosphorus: 58 mg
- Potassium: 91 mg
- Sodium: 72 mg

Preparation Time: 10 minutes

Cooking Time: 30 minutes

Servings: 4

Ingredients:

- 1 lb Thai eggplant (or Japanese or Chinese eggplant)
- 2 tbsp rice vinegar
- 2 tsp sugar
- 1 tsp low-sodium soy sauce
- 1 jalapeño pepper
- 2 garlic cloves
- ¼ cup chopped basil
- Cut vegetables or crackers for serving

Directions:

1. Preheat the oven to 425°F to get it ready. Pierce every eggplant with a skewer or knife. Put on a rimmed baking sheet and cook within 30 minutes. Let it cool, cut in half, and scoop out the flesh of the eggplant into a blender.

2. Add the rice vinegar, sugar, soy sauce, jalapeño, garlic and basil to the blender. Process until smooth. Serve with cut vegetables or crackers.

Nutrition:

- Calories: 40
- Fat: 0 g
- Carbs: 10 g
- Protein: 2 g
- Phosphorus: 34 mg
- Potassium: 284 mg
- Sodium: 47 mg

Preparation Time: 15 minutes

Cooking Time: 8 minutes

Servings: 75 Cookies

Ingredients:

- 5 cups all-purpose flour
- 1 cup + 2 tbsp sugar
- 2 cups butter
- 2 eggs
- 1 tsp almond extract
- 2 tsp vanilla extract

Directions:

1. Preheat your oven to 400°F. Mix butter, flour and sugar together. Put the vanilla almond extract and the eggs.

2. Mix the ingredients using a hand mixer on low speed. Put cookie batter into an ungreased baking sheet. Bake for about 8 minutes. Allow cooling before you serve.

Nutrition:

- Calories: 172
- Carbs: 26 g
- Fat: 0 g
- Phosphorus: 22 mg
- Potassium: 29 mg
- Protein: 2 g
- Sodium: 56 mg

109. Strawberry Pie

Preparation Time: 15 minutes

Cooking Time: 20 minutes

Servings: 8

Ingredients: For the Crust:

- 1 ½ cups Graham cracker crumbs
- 5 tbsp unsalted butter, at room temperature
- 2 tbsp sugar

For the Pie:

- 1 ½ tsp gelatin powder
- 3 tbsp cornstarch
- ¾ cup sugar
- 5 cups sliced strawberries, divided
- 1 cup water

Directions:

1. For the crust: heat your oven to 375°F. Grease a pie pan. Combine the butter, crumbs and sugar, and then press them into your pie pan.

2. Bake the crust for 10 to 15 minutes, until lightly browned. Take it out of the oven and let it cool completely.

3. For the pie, crush up a cup of strawberries. Using a small pot, combine the sugar, water, gelatin and cornstarch. Bring the mixture in the pot up to a boil, lower the heat, and simmer until it has thickened.

4. Add the crushed strawberries into the pot and let it simmer for another 5 minutes until the sauce has thickened up again. Set it off the heat and pour it into a bowl. Cool until it comes to room temperature.

5. Toss the remaining berries with the sauce to be well distributed, pour into the pie crust, and spread it into an even layer. Refrigerate the pie until cold. It will take about 3 hours. Serve and enjoy!

Nutrition:

- Calories: 265
- Protein: 3 g
- Carbs: 48 g
- Fat: 7 g
- Sodium: 143 mg
- Potassium: 183 mg
- Phosphorus. 44 mg

Preparation Time: 10 minutes

Cooking Time: 0 minutes

Servings: 8

Ingredients:

- 1 papaya, peeled, cored, and cut into chunks
- ¼ cup coconut sugar
- ¼ cup pineapple juice
- ⅛ cup mint leaves

Directions:

1. Mix the papaya, coconut sugar, pineapple juice and mint in a mixer until smooth. Chill for 1 hour in the refrigerator.

2. Place the mixture in an ice maker and mix it according to the manufacturer's instructions. Store in an airtight container and freeze for 8 hours or overnight.

Nutrition:

- Calories: 25
- Fat: 0.1 g
- Carbs: 6 g
- Protein: 0.3 g

Preparation Time: 5 minutes

Cooking Time: 8 minutes

Servings: 4

Ingredients:

- 1 cup palm sugar
- 64 oz sugar-free red grapefruit juice
- ½ cup chopped mint
- 2 peeled and cubed grapefruits

Directions:

1. Combine all the fixings into your pot.
2. Cook on low for 8 minutes, then divide into bowls and serve!

Nutrition:

- Calories: 131
- Fat: 4 g
- Carbs: 12 g
- Protein: 2 g

Preparation Time: 15 minutes

Cooking Time: 7 minutes

Servings: 2

Ingredients:

- 1 bowl gelatin cracker crumbs
- ¼ small cup sugar
- ½ cup Unsalted butter

Directions:

1. Mix sweet cracker crumbs, butter and sugar. Put in the oven preheated at 375°F. Bake for 7 minutes, putting it in a greased pie. Let the pie cool before adding any kind of filling. Serve and enjoy!

Nutrition:

- Calories: 205
- Protein: 2 g
- Carbs: 4 g
- Fat: 15 g
- Potassium: 67 mg
- Phosphorus: 22 mg

113. Chocolate Biscotti with Walnuts

Preparation Time: 5 minutes

Cooking Time: 15 minutes

Servings: 12

Ingredients:

- 1 ¼ cups whole-wheat flour
- 1 cup coconut sugar
- 3/2 cup unsweetened cocoa powder
- eggs
- ½ tsp vanilla extract
- ½ tsp baking soda
- ¼ tsp salt
- ½ cup walnuts

Directions:

2. Preheat the oven to 180°C.
3. Mix the ingredients except for the walnuts in a bowl. Mix well with a spoon.
4. Add walnuts until well combined.
5. The dough should be a bit thick and sticky.
6. Place the first half of the dough on a 10 x 15-inch baking sheet coated with nonstick spray. Form a slightly rounded 4-by-12-inch rod about ¾ of an inch thick.
7. Do the same with the second half of the dough. Put it on a second baking sheet and bake for 30 min.
8. Remove the sheets out of the oven and reduce the temperature to 170°C. Let the cookies cool for 20 to 25 min, then cut them into ½-inch-thick slices.
9. Place the cut slices face down on the baking sheet and bake for another 15 min.
10. Flip the cookies to the other side and bake for another 15 min or until very crisp.

Nutrition:

- Calories: 85
- Total Fat: 5.3 g
- Cholesterol: 27 mg
- Sodium: 118 mg
- Total Carbs: 9.9 g
- Dietary Fiber: 4.3 g
- Total Sugars 0.4 g
- Protein: 4.7 g

Preparation Time: 20 minutes

Cooking Time: 20 minutes

Servings: 4

Ingredients:

- ½ cup coconut sugar
- ¼ cup corn-starch
- 1 egg, beaten
- ½ (12 fluid oz) can heavy cream
- ¾ cups coconut milk
- 1 tsp vanilla extract
- ½ (12 oz) package vanilla wafers or your choice
- 2 bananas, sliced

Directions:

1. In a saucepan over medium heat, combine the coconut sugar, potato starch, egg, heavy cream and coconut milk. Mix well and stir until thickened. Remove from the stove, add the vanilla, and mix well.

2. Put a layer of cookies in a large bowl or saucepan. Pour the pudding over the cookies.

3. Garnish it with a layer of banana slices. Place in the refrigerator until it cools.

Nutrition:

- Calories: 261
- Total Fat: 14.2 g
- Cholesterol: 49 mg
- Sodium: 60 mg
- Total Carbs: 31.6 g
- Dietary Fiber: 2.8 g
- Total Sugars: 12.7 g
- Protein: 3.7 g

115. Pecans-Cinnamon Pumpkin Custards

Preparation Time: 10 minutes

Cooking Time: 20 minutes

Servings: 4

Ingredients:

- ½ cup coconut milk
- ½ cup canned pumpkin
- 1 egg, lightly beaten
- ½ cup honey
- ¼ cup refrigerated or frozen egg product (thawed before use)
- 1 tsp vanilla
- ½ tsp ground cinnamon
- ⅛ tsp salt
- ⅛ tsp ground allspice
- ⅛ cup chopped pecans
- ⅛ cup quinoa
- ½ tbsp butter, melted

Directions:

1. Turn the oven to 350°F for preheating. Brush eight 6-oz ramekins with cooking spray. Place the ramekins in two 2-liter square saucepans.

2. Combine coconut milk, pumpkin, eggs, honey, egg products and vanilla in a medium bowl. Sift ½ tsp ground cinnamon, salt and allspice into a small bowl. Add seasoning mix to pumpkin mixture; beat with a whisk until everything is combined.

3. In a small bowl with the spice blend, combine the nuts, quinoa, brown sugar and the remaining ¼ tsp ground cinnamon. Add the melted butter; stir until everything is well combined.

4. Distribute the pumpkin mixture evenly over the prepared dishes. Place the cooking utensils on the rack so that there is enough boiling water in the baking tins up to the middle of the sides of the tins. Bake for 15 minutes.

5. Carefully pour about 1 tbsp of the nut mixture over each. Bake for another 15 to 20 minutes or until a knife comes out clean near the center.

6. Take out the dishes from the water; let them cool on the rack for 30 minutes. Cover and refrigerate for approx 4 hours before serving.

7. To serve, top with whipped dessert and, if desired, sprinkle with freshly grated nutmeg.

Nutrition:

- Calories: 271
- Total Fat: 10.4 g
- Cholesterol: 45 mg
- Sodium: 139 mg
- Total Carbs: 43.3 g
- Dietary Fiber: 2.2 g
- Total Sugars: 37.1 g
- Protein: 4.9 g

Preparation Time: 15 minutes

Cooking Time: 35 minutes

Servings: 8

Ingredients:

- 4 tart apples, pare, core and slice
- ¾ cup sugar
- ½ cup sifted all-purpose flour
- 1/3 cup margarine, softened
- ¾ cup rolled oats
- ¾ tsp nutmeg

Directions:

1. Preheat your oven to 375°F. Place the apples in a greased square 8-inch pan. Mix the other ingredients in a medium-sized bowl and spread the mixture over the apple. Bake within 35 minutes or until the Apple turns lightly brown and tender.

Nutrition:

- Calories: 217
- Carbs: 36 g
- Total Fat: 11g
- Phosphorus: 37 mg
- Potassium: 68 mg
- Protein: 1.4 g
- Sodium: 62 mg

Preparation Time: 15 minutes

Cooking Time: 0 minutes

Servings: 2

Ingredients:

- 2 portions banana cream pudding mix
- 2 ½ cups rice milk
- 8 oz dairy whipped cream
- 12 oz vanilla wafers

Directions:

1. Put vanilla wafers in a pan and, in another bowl, mix banana cream pudding and rice milk. Boil the ingredients while blending them slowly.

2. Pour the mixture over the wafers and make 2 or 3 layers. Put the pan in the fridge for 1 hour and afterward spread the whipped topping over the dessert.

3. Put it back in the refrigerator within 2 hours and serve it cold in transparent glasses. Serve and enjoy!

Nutrition:

- Calories: 255
- Protein: 3 g
- Carbs: 19 g
- Fat: 3 g
- Sodium: 275 mg
- Potassium: 50 mg
- Phosphorus: 40 mg

118. Chocolate Beet Cake

Preparation Time: 15 minutes

Cooking Time: 50 minutes

Servings: 12

Ingredients:

- 3 cups grated beets
- ¼ cup canola oil
- 4 eggs
- 4 oz unsweetened chocolate
- 2 tsp phosphorus-free baking powder
- 2 cups all-purpose flour
- 1 cup sugar

Directions:

1. Set your oven to 325°F. Grease two 8-inch cake pans. Mix the baking powder, flour and sugar. Set aside.

2. Chop the chocolate and dissolve using a double boiler. A microwave can also be used, but don't let it burn.

3. Allow it to cool, and then mix in the oil and eggs. Mix all of the wet fixings into the flour mixture and combine everything until well mixed.

4. Fold the beets in and pour the batter into the cake pans. Let them bake for 40 to 50 minutes. To know it's done, the toothpick should come out clean when inserted into the cake.

5. Remove, then allow them to cool. Once cool, invert over a plate to remove. It is great when served with whipped cream and fresh berries. Enjoy!

Nutrition:

- Calories: 270
- Protein: 6 g
- Carbs: 31 g
- Fat: 17 g
- Sodium: 109 mg
- Potassium: 299 mg
- Phosphorus: 111 mg

119. Pumpkin Cheesecake

Preparation Time: 15 minutes

Cooking Time: 55 minutes

Servings: 2

Ingredients:

- 1 egg white
- 1 wafer crumb, 9-inch pie crust
- ½ small bowl granular sugar
- 1 tsp vanilla extract
- 1 tsp pumpkin pie flavoring
- ½ bowl pumpkin cream
- ½ small bowl liquid egg substitute
- 8 tbsp frozen topping, for desserts
- 16 oz cream cheese

Directions:

1. Brush the pie crust with egg white and cook for 5 minutes in a preheated oven to 375°F and from 375°F down to 350°F.

2. Put sugar, vanilla and cream cheese, beating with a mixer in a large cup until smooth. Beat the egg substitute and add pumpkin cream with pie flavoring; blend everything until softened.

3. Put the pumpkin mixture in a pie shell and bake for 50 minutes to set the center. Then let the pie cool down, and then put it in the fridge. When you wish to, serve it in 8 slices, putting some topping on it. Serve and enjoy!

Nutrition:

- Calories: 364
- Protein: 5 g
- Carbs: 23 g
- Fat: 2 g
- Sodium: 245 mg
- Potassium: 125 mg
- Phosphorus: 65 mg

Preparation Time: 15 minutes

Cooking Time: 1 minute

Servings: 2

Ingredients:

- 1 box angel food cake mix
- 1 box lemon cake mix
- Water
- Nonstick cooking spray or batter
- Dark chocolate small squared chops and chocolate powder

Directions:

1. Use a transparent kitchen cooking bag and put inside both lemon cake mixes, angel food mix, and chocolate squared chops. Mix everything and put water to prepare a small cupcake.

2. Put the mix in a mold to prepare a cupcake containing the ingredients and put it in the microwave for a 1-minute high temperature.

3. Slip the cupcake out of the mold, put it on a dish, let it cool, and put some more chocolate crumbs on it. Serve and enjoy!

Nutrition:

- Calories: 95
- Carbs: 28 g
- Fat: 3 g
- Protein: 1 g
- Sodium: 162 mg
- Potassium: 15 mg
- Phosphorus: 80 mg

Preparation Time: 15 minutes

Cooking Time: 0 minutes

Servings: 2

Ingredients:

- 1-pint whipping cream
- 2 tbsp gelatin
- ½ glass cold water
- 1 glass boiling water
- 3 tbsp lemon juice
- 1 orange glass juice
- 1 tsp sugar
- ¾ cup sliced strawberries
- 1 large angel food cake or light sponge cake

Directions:

1. Put the gelatin in cold water, then add hot water and blend. Add orange and lemon juice, also add some sugar and go on blending. Refrigerate and leave it there until you see it is starting to gel.

2. Whip half a portion of cream, add it to the mixture, and strawberries, put wax paper in the bowl and cut the cake into small pieces.

3. In between the pieces, add the whipped cream and put everything in the fridge for one night. When you take out the cake, add some whipped cream on top and decorate some more fruit. Serve and enjoy!

Nutrition:

- Calories: 355
- Carbs: 15 g
- Fat: 7 g
- Protein: 4 g
- Sodium: 275 mg
- Potassium: 145 mg
- Phosphorus: 145 mg

122. Strawberry Mint Yogurt

Preparation Time: 10 minutes

Cooking Time: 0 minutes

Servings: 4

Ingredients:

- 2 cups non-fat or low-fat plain yogurt
- 1 tbsp organic honey
- 2 cups strawberries, chopped
- 2 tbsp balsamic vinegar
- 2 tbsp mint leaves, finely chopped

Directions:

1. Add together the plain yogurt and organic honey in your small mixing bowl, and mix to combine.

2. In another small mixing bowl, add the chopped strawberries and balsamic vinegar. Use a fork to roughly mash the strawberries in the vinegar, then allow them to rest.

3. Divide the yogurt mixture into serving bowls, and top each with ½ cup of the strawberry mixture and ½ tbsp chopped fresh mint. Serve cold.

Nutrition:

- Calories: 127
- Fat: 2 g
- Carbs: 21 g
- Protein: 7 g

123. Orange Custard Cups

Preparation Time: 4 hours and 20 minutes

Cooking Time: 5 minutes

Servings: 5

Ingredients:

- 3 cups coconut milk, full-fat
- 2 eggs
- ¼ cup fresh orange juice
- 1 medium orange, zested
- 3 scoops intermittent collagen, grass-fed
- 2 tsp vanilla extract, unsweetened
- ⅛ tsp erythritol sweetener
- 1/16 tsp salt
- 1 ½ scoop gelatin, pastured
- 1 cup water

Directions:

1. Place all the ingredients in a food processor except for the gelatin and water, pulse until smooth, then add gelatin and blend until smooth.
2. Divide the custard evenly between 5 half-pint jars and cover with their lid.
3. Switch on the instant pot, pour in water, insert the trivet stand, place the jars on it, and shut the instant pot with its lid in the sealed position.
4. Press the 'manual' button, press '+/-' to set the cooking time to 5 minutes and cook at the high-pressure setting; when the pressure builds in the pot, the cooking timer will start.
5. When the instant pot buzzes, press the 'keep warm' button, do a quick pressure release and open the lid.
6. Carefully remove the jars and let them cool at room temperature for 15 minutes or more until they can be comfortably picked up.
7. Then transfer the custard jars into the refrigerator for a minimum of 4 hours and cool completely.
8. When ready to serve, shake the jars a few times to mix all the ingredients, and then serve.

Nutrition:

- Calories: 250
- Fat: 24 g
- Protein: 5 g
- Net Carbs: 2 g
- Fiber: 3 g

124. Mixed Nut Chocolate Fudge

Preparation Time: 15–30 minutes

Cooking Time: 2 hours 10 minutes

Servings: 4

Ingredients:

- 3 cups unsweetened chocolate chips
- ¼ cup thick coconut milk
- 1 ½ tsp vanilla extract
- A pinch salt
- 1 cup chopped mixed nuts

Directions:

1. Line a 9-inch square pan with baking paper and set aside.
2. Melt the chocolate chips, coconut milk and vanilla in a medium pot over low heat.
3. Mix in the salt and nuts until well distributed and pour the mixture into the square pan.
4. Refrigerate for at least 2 hours.
5. Remove from the fridge, cut into squares, and serve.

Nutrition:

- Calories: 907
- Fat: 31.5 g
- Carbs: 152.1 g
- Protein: 7.7 g

125. Almond Barley Pudding

Preparation Time: 10 minutes

Cooking Time: 25 minutes

Servings: 8

Ingredients:

- 2 cups almond milk
- 1 cup barley
- ½ cup raisins
- ½ cup honey
- 2–3 tsp freshly grated lemon zest
- 1 tsp vanilla extract
- Pinch salt
- Ground cinnamon for dusting (optional)

Directions:

1. Mix almond milk, barley, raisins and honey in a medium-heavy saucepan. Bring to a boil while stirring.

2. Lower the heat and simmer, uncovered, while frequently stirring until the barley is tender and the pudding is creamy within 20 to 25 minutes.

3. Stir almost constantly towards the end to avoid burns. Add the lemon zest, vanilla and salt, and pour the pudding into a bowl or individual bowls. Let cool slightly.

4. Sprinkle with some cinnamon if desired before serving.

Nutrition:

- Calories: 173
- Carbs: 25 g
- Fat: 8 g
- Protein: 3 g

Preparation Time: 10 minutes

Cooking Time: 0 minutes

Servings: 10

Ingredients:

- 5 strawberries, halved
- 1 ½ cantaloupe, cubed
- 2 bananas, cut into chunks
- 1 apple, cored and cut into chunks

Directions:

1. Thread strawberry, cantaloupe, bananas and apple chunks alternately onto skewers.
2. Serve them cold.

Nutrition:

- Calories: 76
- Fat: 1 g
- Carbs: 10 g
- Protein: 2 g

Shopping list

Gallstones cannot be cured, and they can rarely be dissolved naturally. However, despite the fact that they take residence in your gallbladder, you two can get along just fine. Think of it this way. If you feed the gallstones what they want to eat, they will not hurt you. Most gallstones never show symptoms. To make sure that it will stay that way, you have to follow a healthy and balanced diet that will not only keep your gallbladder from getting irritated but will also be beneficial for the rest of your body.

So, forget the aisles where the chips and chocolate hide, and fill your shopping cart with some of these Ingredients:

Unrefined and Healthy Fats

Including healthy fats in your diet, such as olive oil and coconut oil, can make a significant difference in the health of your gallbladder. Coconut oil most likely contains the most easily digestible healthy fats known as medium-chained fatty acids. Extra-virgin olive oil, in particular, contains anti-inflammatory properties that can help your gallstones pass and, in some cases, dissolve. That is why there are far fewer registered patients with gallstones in countries where olive oil is widely consumed, such as the Mediterranean.

Foods High in Fiber

Fiber is an extremely important macronutrient that is known to aid digestion, which your body desperately requires at this point. Make an effort to consume 30 to 40 grams of fiber per day. This will not only prevent new gallstones from forming but will also prevent existing gallstones from growing and causing pain. All types of nuts, beans, and legumes are welcome.

Many people believe that eating these will cause gas and irritation in the gallbladder, but this is not true. If you soak your beans and legumes and sprout your nuts and seeds, your body will digest them easily and you will still get all of the essential nutrients.

Whole-Grains

There is no healthy diet that does not include whole grains, so make sure your gallstone diet does as well. Whole grains are high in fiber, which helps to prevent gallstone formation. Fiber is known to have the ability to bind with cholesterol and bile, speeding up the removal process.

Fruits and Vegetables That Are Raw

Raw fruits and vegetables are naturally high in antioxidants, water, and electrolytes while being low in unhealthy fats and salts, so they should be the foundation of your gallstone diet. No, I am not suggesting that you become a vegetarian; however, increasing your intake of raw and plant-based ingredients is the key to allowing your gallbladder to function properly despite the presence of gallstones.

Choose antioxidant-rich ingredients that have detoxifying effects, support the health of your liver, and aid in the breakdown of fat cells, such as artichokes, beets, dandelion leaves, and so on.

Potassium-rich foods should also be on your menu. Avocados, dark leafy greens, bananas, sweet potatoes, tomatoes, and other similar foods are both delicious and beneficial in the treatment of gallstones.

Foods High in Lean Protein

Including protein in your diet is important, but when you have gallstones and want to keep the symptoms and pain at bay, you must be careful about the type of protein you consume. People who have gallstones should choose lean protein sources that are also organic. Skinless chicken, turkey, wild-caught fish, organic protein powder, lean red meat in moderation, and so on are examples.

Fish and seafood are a healthy addition to the gallstone diet, but they must be consumed with caution. Shellfish such as lobster, shrimp, crab, scallops, and others are extremely low in fat and therefore ideal for people suffering from gallstones. If you have gallstones, limit or avoid eating fatty fish like salmon, tuna, and trout, and instead eat low-fat fish like haddock, cod, pollock, flounder, orange roughy, and so on. If you have asymptomatic gallstones, you can eat fatty fish on occasion.

No Fat, No Hurt!

A high-fat diet can even cause discomfort in a healthy person. Consider how harsh it would be for someone suffering from digestive organ disease. A person whose gallbladder has gallstones is unable to function normally. A high-fat diet will not only cause discomfort, but it may also cause severe pain and necessitate the removal of the patients' gallbladders.

To avoid all of this and allow your gallbladder to function normally despite the presence of gallstones, you must reduce your fat intake and the fat cells that should be broken down by your digestive organs.

This will not cure your gallbladder, but it will help it function properly and prevent gallstone attacks and acute pain.

And, because I know that breaking old habits is easier said than done, I've compiled a list of general fat-loss tips:

- Prepare your meals from scratch. That is the only way to know exactly what and how much is in your meals. This gives you control over your fat consumption and a fairly accurate picture of how much you consume.

- Always read labels before purchasing. Look for foods that are low in fat rather than reduced in fat. Reduced fat may imply a 20% reduction in fat content, but it does not imply that the product is no longer fatty.

- Reduce your consumption of red milk. For example, if you're making spaghetti Bolognese, you can cut the milk in half and replace it with pureed beans in the sauce.

- When cooking, do not pour oil, but rather measure it. As a general rule, 1 tsp of fat or oil per person is recommended.

- Purchase a cooking spray or simply fill a clean spray bottle with olive oil. This will force you to cook with as little oil as possible.

- Do not add more oil if the meat becomes stuck to the bottom of the pan. A drop or two of water will assist you in scraping up the burnt pieces without increasing the fat content.

- Before cooking, remove all visible skin and fat from the meat.

- When making stews or casseroles, remove the fat from the top.

- Food should not be fried. Instead, bake, boil, grill, steam, or roast.

- Instead of mayonnaise, make your own low-fat dressings with fresh herbs, lemon juice, and low-fat yogurt.

Without a doubt, the gallbladder is not required to keep your body running and healthy. Most people are unaware that gallstones are forming. Remember that gallstones can cause a variety of symptoms such as vomiting, nausea, bloating, and abdominal pain. The symptoms could be recurring and frequent. The final option is surgery to remove this organ.

Gender and family history are two risk factors that contribute to the development of gallstones. Women are more likely than men to develop gallstones. Obesity increases the likelihood of gallstone formation, so body weight is an important consideration. Furthermore, a low-fiber and high-fat diet may be the main culprit. You can avoid gallbladder problems by changing your diet.

If you are obese, make sure to gradually lose weight. Quick weight loss should be avoided because it can lead to gallstone formation. Crash diets cause the liver to produce extra cholesterol in bile, disrupting your hormonal balance. The extra cholesterol may crystallize and form gallstones.

To keep your gallbladder healthy, eat a well-balanced diet that includes lean meats, vegetables, fiber, and fruits. Fresh vegetables and fiber-rich fruits are essential for your body. The diet must reduce the gallbladder's stress. Legumes, spices, nuts, whole grains, low-fat dairy products, vegetables, and fresh fruits are examples of healthy foods.

Conversion Table

American and British Variances

Term	Abbreviation	Nationality	Dry or liquid	Metric equivalent	Equivalent in context
cup	c., C.		usually liquid	237 milliliters	16 tablespoons or 8 ounces
ounce	fl oz, fl. oz.	American	liquid only	29.57 milliliters	
		British	either	28.41 milliliters	
gallon	gal.	American	liquid only	3.785 liters	4 quarts
		British	either	4.546 liters	4 quarts
inch	in, in.			2.54 centimeters	
ounce	oz, oz.	American	dry	28.35 grams	1/16 pound
			liquid	see OUNCE	see OUNCE
pint	p., pt.	American	liquid	0.473 liter	1/8 gallon or 16 ounces
			dry	0.551 liter	1/2 quart
		British	either	0.568 liter	
pound	lb.		dry	453.592 grams	16 ounces
Quart	q., qt, qt.	American	liquid	0.946 liter	1/4 gallon or 32 ounces
			dry	1.101 liters	2 pints
		British	either	1.136 liters	
Teaspoon	t., tsp., tsp		either	about 5 milliliters	1/3 tablespoon
Tablespoon	T., tbs., tbsp.		either	about 15 milliliters	3 teaspoons or 1/2 ounce

Volume (Liquid)

American Standard (Cups & Quarts)	American Standard (Ounces)	Metric (Milliliters & Liters)
2 tbsp.	1 fl. oz.	30 ml
1/4 cup	2 fl. oz.	60 ml
1/2 cup	4 fl. oz.	125 ml
1 cup	8 fl. oz.	250 ml
1 1/2 cups	12 fl. oz.	375 ml
2 cups or 1 pint	16 fl. oz.	500 ml
4 cups or 1 quart	32 fl. oz.	1000 ml or 1 liter
1 gallon	128 fl. oz.	4 liters

Volume (Dry)

American Standard	Metric
1/8 teaspoon	5 ml
1/4 teaspoon	1 ml
1/2 teaspoon	2 ml
3/4 teaspoon	4 ml
1 teaspoon	5 ml
1 tablespoon	15 ml
1/4 cup	59 ml
1/3 cup	79 ml
1/2 cup	118 ml
2/3 cup	158 ml
3/4 cup	177 ml
1 cup	225 ml
2 cups or 1 pint	450 ml
3 cups	675 ml
4 cups or 1 quart	1 liter
1/2 gallon	2 liters
1 gallon	4 liters

Oven Temperatures

American Standard	Metric
250° F	130° C
300° F	150° C
350° F	180° C
400° F	200° C
450° F	230° C

Weight (Mass)

American Standard (Ounces)	Metric (Grams)
1/2 ounce	15 grams
1 ounce	30 grams
3 ounces	85 grams
3.75 ounces	100 grams
4 ounces	115 grams
8 ounces	225 grams
12 ounces	340 grams
16 ounces or 1 pound	450 grams

Dry Measure Equivalents

3 teaspoons	1 tablespoon	1/2 ounce	14.3 grams
2 tablespoons	1/8 cup	1 ounce	28.3 grams
4 tablespoons	1/4 cup	2 ounces	56.7 grams
5 1/3 tablespoons	1/3 cup	2.6 ounces	75.6 grams
8 tablespoons	1/2 cup	4 ounces	113.4 grams
12 tablespoons	3/4 cup	6 ounces	.375 pound
32 tablespoons	2 cups	16 ounces	1 pound

Conclusion

Thank you for reading this book. When you develop gallstones and are forced to have your gallbladder out, you're less likely to take the health of your digestive tract for granted.

People frequently overlook the importance of the gallbladder because they are unaware of its function. Without the gallbladder, the biliary system cannot function. It is in charge of bile storage, transport, and production. Bile, which is required for digestion, is produced by the liver. This bile is stored in your gallbladder until it is needed by your body.

Your body is an incredible machine. It is resilient and adaptable, so you should be able to live a healthy and fulfilling life without a gallbladder. It may take some time to adjust to the dietary changes that come with gallbladder removal, but your body will adapt in the end.

However, it's critical to keep a close eye on your digestion and notify your doctor if you experience any persistent digestive symptoms. Consult your doctor right away if you have abdominal pain, fever, vomiting, or worsening diarrhea.

Take care of yourself in addition to your diet. Get outside and take a walk in the woods. The movement aids in weight loss, aerobic fitness, flexibility, and stress relief.

Some people may be required to undergo cholecystectomy surgery for a variety of reasons, including health concerns. Many questions about this situation arise frequently, and one of the most common is what to eat without a gallbladder. Make it a point to show your digestive tract love and attention from now on by eating healthy whole foods and keeping a journal in which you document any symptoms you experience so you can adjust your diet accordingly.

Best of luck and best of health in the future!